Responding to CYBER BULLYING

I dedicate this book to my son Kole, whose excitement for knowledge keeps me seeking the wonderments of life. May we always search for solutions and great wisdom.

—Jill Joline Myers

I dedicate this book to two outstanding people: my best friend and husband Mark, and my mom Hiroko Mettler. My mom's active mind, love for learning, and youthful energy have always inspired me toward greater levels of excellence.

—Donna S. McCaw

A special dedication to the special people in my life: my best friend and husband Hoyet, my father, my children, and my grand baby. You are my inspiration and reason to live.

—Leaunda S. Hemphill

Responding to CYBER BULLYING

An Action Tool for School Leaders

Jill Joline Myers
Donna S. McCaw
Leaunda S. Hemphill

For information:

Corwin
A SAGE Company
2455 Teller Road
Thousand Oaks, California 91320
(800) 233-9936
Fax: (800) 417-2466
www.corwin.com

SAGE India Pvt. Ltd.
B 1/I 1 Mohan Cooperative
Industrial Area
Mathura Road,
New Delhi 110 044
India

SAGE Ltd.
1 Oliver's Yard
55 City Road
London EC1Y 1SP
United Kingdom

SAGE Asia-Pacific Pte. Ltd.
33 Pekin Street #02-01
Far East Square
Singapore 048763

Printed in the United States of America

Library of Congress Cataloging-in-Publication Data

Myers, Jill J.
Responding to cyber bullying : an action tool for school leaders / Jill J. Myers, Donna S. McCaw, Leaunda S. Hemphill.
p. cm.
Includes bibliographical references and index.
ISBN 978-1-4129-9484-2 (pbk.)
1. Cyberbullying. 2. Bullying in schools. 3. School violence. I. McCaw, Donna. II. Hemphill, Leaunda S. III. Title.

LB3013.3.M94 2011
371.5′8—dc22 2010040679

This book is printed on acid-free paper.

10 11 12 13 14 10 9 8 7 6 5 4 3 2 1

Acquisitions Editor: Debra Stollenwerk
Associate Editor: Desirée A. Bartlett
Editorial Assistant: Kimberly Greenberg
Production Editor: Melanie Birdsall
Copy Editor: Cate Huisman
Typesetter: C&M Digitals (P) Ltd.
Proofreader: Kate Peterson
Indexer: Sheila Bodell
Cover Designer: Karine Hovsepian
Permissions Editor: Karen Ehrmann

Brief Contents

Additional materials and resources related to *Responding to Cyber Bullying: An Action Tool for School Leaders* can be found at www.corwin.com/cyberbullying

Detailed Contents

Additional materials and resources related to *Responding to Cyber Bullying: An Action Tool for School Leaders* can be found at www.corwin.com/cyberbullying

Preface

This manual is dedicated to the competing principles (1) that schools are not required to surrender control over school activities to students and (2) that students are exposed to a robust exchange of ideas.[1] While the classroom needs to be a *marketplace of ideas* where First Amendment free expression exists, a safe and orderly school environment conducive to learning must be maintained. The increasing use of technologies, including the Internet, the most participatory form of mass speech yet developed,[2] confounds administrative decision making. Technology use muddles the point at which students' First Amendment protections end and a school's authority begins. The schoolyard may no longer be confined within its physical limitations.

This manual provides public school leaders and front-line school personnel with data-driven solutions for resolving cyber bullying incidents. Included within the manual are the following:

1. Comprehensive and easily applied tests that differentiate netiquette violations from First Amendment protected expressions.
2. Strategies for school leaders to use to address and document aggressive cyber situations.
3. Real-world cyber bullying scenarios from court cases that address the authority of schools to regulate, censor, or sanction inappropriate cyber expression by students both on and off campus.
4. The cyber bullying School Sanctioning Worksheet that provides practical guidelines for school decision makers. These guidelines support transparent accountability, identify specific and objective factors for school personnel to assess in each case, and document a school's decision to sanction cyber bullying incidents.

The primary focus of this manual concerns school leaders' decision-making processes when dealing with incidents of cyber bullying. The real-world examples provided will equip school administrators with the knowledge and tools to lead their schools or districts through issues surrounding cyber bullying. It should be noted, however, that *although differences between cyber bullying and bullying exist, these materials may also be used when dealing with other bullying or discipline issues*. The suggestions included in this handbook may easily be applied to other student disciplinary decisions.

The book is organized into four sections. The Introduction discusses cyber bullying as a recent, emerging phenomenon. Cyber bullying is defined within the context of appropriate school behavior. Examples of sexting and slamming support the statistical significance of the problem in public education. This section raises the challenges to school districts created by students' inappropriate use of technology. A brief summary of current state remedies is also discussed.

The next section of the book is titled Part I, Resolving School Cyber Situations. This section is divided into nine chapters that provide a brief update on recent court cases related to cyber bullying and public school safety. The purpose of this section is to provide a complete legal analysis of cyber bullying situations through the eyes of the courts. Case scenarios provide real-life examples of student expressions that are both terrifying and destructive to productive school functioning. The case discussions impart a strong foundation for making legally sound decisions, and they include the dictates of the courts regarding a school's duty to protect its students from harm.

Chapter 1 identifies the issues and confusions existing in schools resulting from student cyber expressions. This chapter distinguishes protected expressions from unprotected expressions as this distinction is reflected in court decisions. Chapter 2 reviews the Supreme Court's perception of appropriate student expressions at school. It provides the three categories of student expression that can be controlled by school administrators. Chapter 3 discusses the state and local take on school-related expressions. Highlights of regional differences in resolving cyber bullying issues in schools are discussed. Too often, school administrators believe that the concept of *in loco parentis* authorizes total control of students while under school supervision. This is, in fact, no longer true. Public schools no longer act in the place of parents.

Chapter 4 focuses on inappropriate student expressions that are vulgar, lewd, or developmentally unacceptable for the intended student audience. Chapter 5 examines the school official's ability to control pedagogy and school-authorized academic and extracurricular activities, publications, and events. Chapter 6 details disruptive student expressions that impact the educational environment. This includes expressions that disrupt by implying that there will be violence, causing administrative management issues, or undermining school leadership authority.

Chapter 7 addresses a school's authority to reach beyond the schoolyard gate. Off-campus activities that establish a sufficient nexus (connection) to school-related functions may be censored provided that they substantially disrupt the school or impede students from obtaining educational benefits. Chapter 8 focuses on a school's duty to protect from peer-on-peer cyber bullying. A school is not responsible for peer-on-peer activity *unless* the school is aware of the situation and is deliberately indifferent to the circumstances. Even then, the school would not be responsible for the harm *unless* a pattern of systemic abuse has occurred. Chapter 9 covers proactive approaches that have been developed to deal with school cyber bullying situations. These approaches include state and federal legislative mandates, community practices, and school-parent-student acceptable use policies.

Part II examines the basic lessons and rules school administrators need to know to avoid liability for or litigation from inappropriately responding to cyber bullying situations. This part discusses the schools' options while handling these incidents and the schools' need to provide fact-intensive justification for its actions. This section is divided into two chapters. Chapter 10 discusses the lessons learned from decisions that school personnel have made in the past. In particular, this chapter demonstrates how costly cyber censoring mistakes are to school districts, and it lists options other than censorship that are available to schools. Chapter 11 summarizes the Top Ten Rules that generally govern school authority over student cyber expressions. These Rules stem from Supreme Court decisions and the lower courts' interpretations thereof. The Top Ten Rules give school officials concise guidance regarding which student expressions can be regulated and which cannot.

Part III gives the reader the tools needed to systematically evaluate and determine appropriate cyber bullying disciplinary actions. Chapter 12 introduces the MATRIX, a rubric that will assist administrators in formulating decisions that are *not* arbitrary and capricious. The chapter describes the need for such a decision-making tool and identifies the philosophical goals that support its use. Chapter 13 describes in detail how the MATRIX works. Included within this chapter is a sanctioning worksheet organized into six sections.

Each section identifies specific information relevant to school discipline. The six sections are

Section 1: The student/offender's pedigree information, general background information, and contact information for those involved in the incident.

Section 2: The category and description of the cyber bullying presenting offense.

Section 3: Numerical calculations correlating to the intensity of the presenting offense.

Section 4: Numerical calculations correlating to the offender's status and personal characteristics.

Section 5: Numerical calculations mitigating the offender's liability for his or her conduct.

Section 6: The total sanctioning score and actual disposition received.

A step-by-step description for completing the worksheet provides a straightforward guide with which to process and document a school's sanctioning decisions.

CAVEAT

The manual and accompanying MATRIX provide an objective framework within which to structure a sanctioning decision. The manual does not dictate specific sanctions and should be used as a guide only. This material is advisory, and its use is voluntary. School administrators must consider what is an appropriate sanction based on community standards, the policies of regional offices of education, and specific state legislative directives. If any discrepancies arise between school or state policies and the manual's recommendations, always defer to independent legal counsel. Decisions to act or refrain from acting should not be determined on the basis of this information without seeking legal advice. The manual is intended to complement a school district's preexisting decision-making practices, not to replace them.

Notes

1. Tinker v. Des Moines Independent Community School District, 393 U.S. 503, 512 (1969).
2. Reno v. ACLU, 521 U.S. 844, 863 (1997).

Acknowledgments

Corwin gratefully acknowledges the following individuals for their editorial insight:

Margarete Couture, Principal
South Seneca Central School District
Interlaken, NY

Laurie Emery, Principal
Old Vail Middle School
Vail, AZ

David Freitas, Professor
Indiana University South Bend
South Bend, IN

Jill Gildea, Superintendent
Fremont School District 79
Mundelein, IL

Barb Keating, Principal
New Westminster School District
Lord Kelvin Community School
New Westminster, BC, Canada

About the Authors

Jill Joline Myers has extensive experience dealing with juvenile offenders through the criminal court system. In two decades as a state prosecuting attorney, she dealt with a wide spectrum of inappropriate and illegal behaviors, from school truancy to terrorism. As an associate professor at Western Illinois University teaching criminal justice courses, she is aware of the need for a straightforward, transparent, consistent, and nonbiased sanctioning process. Her research agenda includes civil liability of state agents, violence reduction strategies, and cyber bullying. She regularly instructs state and federal agencies on constitutional issues.

Donna S. McCaw's three decades in public schools include experience in special education services and school counseling as well as positions as school principal and director of curriculum. Currently, she serves as a professor of educational leadership at Western Illinois University. In that capacity she teaches at the master's and doctoral levels. Her specialties include issues and challenges surrounding effective 21st-century leadership. In addition to a love of teaching, she has a commitment to work with public schools. Consequently, through her school consulting work, she spends much time guiding and directing improvement processes.

Over the past 20 years, Leaunda S. Hemphill has consulted with higher education and K–12 faculty on the use of effective instruction in computer-based and online environments. As an associate professor at Western Illinois University, she teaches instructional design and K–12 technology integration courses in the Instructional Design and Technology Department. She also teaches online student assessment for Illinois Online Network. She regularly conducts professional development workshops for state and international organizations. Her research includes evaluating online instruction and interactivity, and integrating emerging online technologies and virtual environments into the classroom.

Introduction

The Digital Generation Expresses Itself

Today's students have a great deal of technological sophistication. They have embraced cyber technology and digital media as a lifestyle for communicating, making cultural connections, interacting, and social networking. In fact, given their obsession with technology, this generation of children is commonly referred to as the "Net Generation"[1] or the "Digital Generation."

Children use cyber technology to easily communicate with their friends locally and globally. Students also share their thoughts, culture, and information instantaneously over mobile devices. World events, scientific breakthroughs, and information on every conceivable subject are available by surfing the Internet. Other Internet services provide guidance; find people; locate products; and purchase supplies, music, and tickets. A requirement for student success in the 21st century, the Internet is a necessary tool for researching and gathering resources for the completion of school assignments. The prevalence of available technologies and the pervasiveness of Internet use are steadily growing. Preteenagers and adolescents increasingly use these technologies to send text messages and participate in social networks.

Figure I.1 illustrates the increasing reliance on digital media by teens ages 12 to 17 to communicate online.[2] Just because cyber kids have fully embraced technology does not mean they have the maturity to properly use it. Although technology has brought advantages in communication, information, and entertainment from the world to the fingertips of students, it has also brought with it certain disadvantages: Identity theft, online predators, pornographic displays, viral attacks, and spamming[3] are commonly mentioned. Another emergent disadvantage of digital media is that it provides easy and convenient opportunities for students to harass, humiliate, or bully others online. Its convenience, demonstrated usage, and accessibility should not give children the green light to employ cyber technology as they see fit. Nor should technology empower students with an absolute freedom to lambaste their peers or the school administration. Unfortunately, that is exactly what is happening.

Figure I.1 Pew Internet and American Life Project Survey Results (summarized from Lenhart, Madden, MacGill, & Smith, 2007[4])

Activity	Percentage of Students Ages 12–17 Using This Technology in 2004	Percentage of Students Ages 12–17 Using This Technology in 2007
Share artwork, photos, videos, or stories online	33	39
Create work on web pages or blogs for others	32	33
Create online journal or blog	19	28
Maintain personal webpage	22	27
Remix online content into their own creations	19	26
Create a profile on a social networking site		55
Upload photos to Internet site		47
Post a video online		14

Once cyber bullying occurs, the results can quickly creep into the classroom, where students eventually face the consequences. Teachers and administrators feel compelled to respond. Most children are not emotionally equipped to effectively control the situation, nor do they have the technological savvy. They cannot escape the collateral damages to their psyches or to their reputations. Therefore, teachers and administrators often step in to resolve the situation. They typically respond to cyber aggression by offering solutions and/or developing programs for mitigating its occurrences.

As cyber bullying incidents increasingly affect educational institutions, school personnel must prepare to meet the challenge. Yet they struggle with their role, their legal authority to intervene, the decision to censor communications by minors, and disciplinary decision making. It is vital that school personnel clearly understand their role in protecting students from harm while promoting free exchange of ideas. Enforcing cyber bullying policies cannot come at the expense of constitutional free speech rights. The challenge is in understanding the difference and applying the appropriate response within the schoolyard gates. It is this struggle that this handbook seeks to address.

Cyber Bullying: An All-Encompassing Definition

Before addressing the response to student inappropriate cyber expressions, it is important to note the scope and depth of the problem. The National Crime Prevention Council defines the issue as follows: "Online bullying, called cyber bullying, happens when teens use the Internet, cell phones, or other devices to send or post text or images intended to hurt or embarrass another person."[5] Patchin and Hinduja define cyber bullying as the "willful and repeated harm inflicted through the medium of electronic text."[6] Thus, the definition includes bullying through e-mail, instant messaging (IM), social networking websites, chat rooms, and digital messages or images sent to computers, cellular phones, or handheld communication devices.[7] Cyber bullying or electronic aggression occurs when a child, preteen, or teen is tormented, threatened, harassed, humiliated, embarrassed, or otherwise targeted by another child.[8] Simply stated, cyber bullying occurs when a minor uses electronic communication technology to bully others.[9]

All of the definitions cover a broad range of conduct. Cyber bullying includes malicious intent, repetitious mistreatment, or a chronic pattern of abuse over time via open direct attacks or indirect contacts causing social isolation and exclusion.[10]

Methods of Exploitation

The methods used by students to electronically bully others are extensive and limited only by the children's imagination and access to the technology. The methodology involves knowledge of a language unique to cyber savvy individuals. Children now "flame," "out," "phish," "bash," "spam," "impersonate," poll, and "sext" each other. They also mock, harass, parody, and threaten in a high-tech manner. The technology provides a new platform to bully, tease, target, and torment. Some of the more common techniques used to bully include the following:

1. *Flaming.* Online fighting by posting or sending an extremely critical or abusive electronic mail message in a public forum to inflame or enrage the recipient, often as retaliation to a perceived slight.[11]
2. *Outing and phishing.* Engaging a victim in an IM conversation that tricks the victim into revealing sensitive or confidential information, and then forwarding this revelation to others as a "joke."[12]
3. *Using "bash boards."* Posting racist remarks and gossip to online forums.[13]
4. *Spamming.* Sending unwanted and unsolicited e-mails in bulk that may obstruct the entire system in an attempt to force the message on people who would not otherwise choose to receive it.[14]
5. *Impersonating.* Hacking into a victim's account and then sending messages that contain embarrassing or insulting information while masquerading as the victim to damage a friendship or reputation.[15]
6. *Sending hate mail.* Sending messages designed to play on prejudices, including biases about race and sex.[16]
7. *Cyber stalking.* Sending messages that contain threats of harm or messages that are highly intimidating, causing victims to fear for their safety.[17]
8. *Harassing.* Repeatedly sending offensive, rude, and insulting messages.[18]
9. *Denigrating.* "Dissing" (disrespecting) someone online—posting cruel statements, gossip, or rumors to destroy or damage a reputation.[19]
10. *Sexting.* Taking an embarrassing sexually explicit photo and posting it on the Internet.
11. *Threatening.* Deliberately posting a statement that indicates harm to another.[20]
12. *Anonymizing.* Using an anonymizer, an intermediary website, that hides or disguises the IP address associated with the

Internet user. Generally these sites allow a person to engage in various Internet activities without leaving an easily traceable digital footprint.[21]

13. *Polling.* Establishing virtual polling places online to enable fellow students to vote on undesirable characteristics, such as which student is the fattest, ugliest, sluttiest, geekiest, and so forth.[22]
14. *Exclusion or boycott.* Intentionally excluding a person from an online group, a chat room, a game, or an IM buddies list.[23]
15. *Trolling.* Intentionally posting provocative messages about sensitive subjects to create conflict, upset people, and bait them into "flaming" or fighting.[24]
16. *Cyber bullying by proxy.* Convincing others to send flame or hate mail to the victim and then, when the victim responds, forwarding responses to an authority figure who then punishes the victim.
17. *Poking.* Reaching out and virtually touching someone online. Basically when a friend is poked on a social network site like Facebook, MySpace, or Bebo, the person receives a message notifying them of the contact. Not all pokes are harmless.[25]
18. *Happy slapping.* Intentionally provoking an unwitting individual into a physical altercation with a tormentor(s). An accomplice videotapes or photographs the attack, typically using a camera cell phone. The perpetrators then post the video online. The victim does not realize the event was captured electronically.[26]

Common Examples

Examples of these methods of cyber bullying appear in court cases and news reports. For example, denigrating and polling significantly affected one 15-year-old student's life. The child privately filmed himself dancing around his bedroom portraying a *Star Wars* character wielding a pretend light saber. Inadvertently the child left his videotape at school, where other students uploaded it online and invited viewers to make insulting remarks about the clip. The popularity of the two-minute *Star Wars Kid* video resulted in over 15 million hits and over 106 clone video productions.[27] The vicious comments resulting from the dissemination were so mortifying that the child dropped out of school and finished the semester in a children's psychiatric ward.

According to the statement of charges in the lawsuit that was filed, the teenager claimed that the fallout from the posting "was simply unbearable, totally. It was impossible to attend class."[28]

A recent Florida case demonstrated how happy slapping affected a young cheerleader. She was knocked unconscious, suffered from a concussion, and experienced severe bruising around her head. The beating was so severe that her father did not recognize her. The case involved six teenagers heinously attacking a schoolmate. The purpose of the attack was to create video content for posting to YouTube. After luring her into a private home, they took turns hitting her, screaming at her—all the while videotaping the incident. One offender was recorded saying, "Make this 17 seconds good."[29]

Sexting is another increasingly popular method of cyber bullying among high school students. Twenty percent[30] to 30%[31] of teenagers report some level of engagement in the activity. In 2008, the National Campaign to Prevent Teen and Unplanned Pregnancy and CosmoGirl commissioned a survey to quantify the number of teens and young adults who post sexually suggestive text or nude or seminude photos, videos, or images.[32] Their results indicated that overall 20% of all teens engage in this conduct. A breakdown of their results further revealed that 22% of teen girls, 18% of teen boys, and 11% of young teen girls (ages 13–16) self-reported participating in the activity. Unfortunately, serious consequences have resulted from participating in sexting. Criminal child pornography charges have been filed. If convicted, the child offenders are required to register as sex offenders. Some schools report suspending the sexting offenders. A most disturbing outcome of such cyber aggression has been the suicides of two children.[33]

Sexting is becoming a greater social concern. Educators, law enforcement agencies, and lawmakers are now exploring alternative ways to control the use of cell phones for sexual interaction and exploitation. Criminal prosecution of the conduct under current statutes results in harsh consequences. Prosecution stigmatizes youth for long periods of time because of sexual offender registration requirements and limited employment possibilities. Less punitive alternatives are being explored.

Calibrated responses are under discussion in a number of state legislatures. Vermont is considering exempting a child from child pornography prosecution when the juvenile offender voluntarily transmits or receives his or her own image. However, the conduct could still be prosecuted under lesser charges, such as for lewd and lascivious conduct or for disseminating indecent materials to a minor. In a similar vein, Ohio is weighing whether to make juvenile sexting a first-degree misdemeanor offense, thus distinguishing juvenile offenders from adult offenders, who would be prosecuted as felons.[34] Kentucky is mulling over levying fines on teens caught sexting. Illinois is considering adding alternative responses to its child pornography law. Specifically, Illinois lawmakers are contemplating mandating counseling, community service, and other responses in lieu of incarceration if a minor engages in sexting.[35] As these various responses indicate, all agree that the conduct needs to be addressed. How to handle it is the rub; should it be through prosecution, decriminalization, treatment, education, or something else?

Statistical Evidence of the Problem

As is evidenced by the variety of techniques mentioned above, cyber bullying is different from traditional bullying. Cyber bullying differs in the method of victimization. It also differs in that it can happen 24 hours a day and seven days a week. Technology affords new platforms for abuse and amplifies its negative effects. Clearly, cyber bullying reaches beyond the schoolyard. Cyber bullying affords the bully a veil of anonymity, instantaneous access to the victim, and an unlimited audience of bystanders and supporters. The victim cannot escape the digital message disseminated by the tormentor.

A review by TopTenREVIEWS of the most popular social networking websites revealed six sites that were available free to children under 16.[36] Five of the six sites allowed children as young as 13 to join. MySpace was the exception, setting its minimum age at 14. The percentage of minors and others reported using these websites was considerable. The potential for inappropriate contact and access by strangers and predators was apparent. Only the Bebo site made profiles "private" automatically upon creation. (For the others, newly created profiles were automatically made public, and extra steps were necessary to keep information private.) However, the Bebo site did not further limit its "private" option to individuals whom users had identified as "friends" or to the friends of such identified friends.

All sites have the capacity for creating safety precautions. Protection is afforded by allowing users to limit access to those they choose on an individual basis or allowing them to set minimum and maximum ages of those who may view their accounts. It's open to question how many children comprehend the risks, are tech savvy enough to manually alter the default settings, and actually take the time to adjust them. Figure I.2 summarizes the extent of participation by children in social networking websites.

Figure I.2 Child Participation in Social Networking Websites

Website	Total Number of Users	Popularity Ranking	Minimum Age	Percentage of Those Using Website Who Are Minors
Facebook	93,300,000 unique monthly visitors[37]	1	13	36
MySpace	61,300,000 unique monthly visitors[38]	2	14	33
Bebo	5,400,000 unique monthly visitors[39]	3	13	54
Friendster	2,400,000 unique monthly visitors[40]	4	16	3
hi5	4,100,000 unique monthly visitors[41]	5	13	24
Orcut	475,000 unique monthly visitors[42]	6	18	4
Perfspot	user numbers unavailable	7	13	32
Yahoo! 360	Shut down July 13, 2009[43]	8	18	16
Zorpia	83,975 downloads[44]	9	16	15
Netlog (popular in Europe)	35,000,000 registered users[45]	10	13	31

Cyber aggression interferes with student learning. It also prevents students from achieving their potential. The injury is usually intangible but includes loss of reputation, loss of associations, and intentional infliction of emotional distress. Often cyber aggression leaves the victim feeling humiliated, threatened, and powerless.[46] Children who are bullied, teased, harassed, or ostracized are not the only victims. The climate of disrespect and fear created by cyber aggression also affects bystanders, family members, teachers, and administrators. Results include educational losses, mental and physical health issues, and lost productivity.

A 2001 national survey reported that the inappropriate usage of technology is problematic to more 8- to 15-year-olds than issues concerning violence, drug and alcohol usage, racism, or the pressures to have sex.[47] Fifty-five percent of 8- to 11-year-olds reported bullying and teasing as their biggest problem, whereas only 46% reported violence as a big problem, 44% reported alcohol or drugs as a big problem, and 33 % reported pressure to have sex as a big problem. Somewhat similarly, 68% of 12- to 15-year-olds reported bullying and teasing as their biggest problem, 68% identified alcohol or drugs as a big problem, 62% reported violence as a big problem, and 49% reported pressure to have sex as a big problem.

So how does this biggest problem relate or connect to schools, school administrators, teachers, and staff? The extent of electronic aggression is now so alarming that the Centers for Disease Control and Prevention recognize it as an emergent health risk affecting nearly 75% of teenagers between the ages of 12 and 17.[48] Furthermore, according to a 2008 California study, of the 75% who were bullied online, 85% had been bullied at school, and 51% of them reported that the bullying was done by schoolmates.[49]

Other studies found a minimum of 9% to 35% of all school-aged children[50] and 42% to 53% of children in fourth through eighth grades[51] have been cyber bullying victims. Every day, 160,000 children miss school because they fear bullying.[52] Worse yet, although all bullying behavior has been identified as increasing suicidal ideation, cyber bullying is reportedly a stronger predictor of suicidal thoughts than regular bullying. Cyber bullying victims are almost twice as likely to have attempted suicide as youth who have not experienced cyber bullying.[53]

A 2009 survey conducted by the Associated Press (AP) and MTV reported the potential for even more gruesome consequences if young victims are involved.[54] The AP-MTV study found that middle school victims of cyber bullying are more apt to commit suicide than are all other victims. Significantly, the study found that 8% of cyber bullying victims and 12% of sexting victims have considered ending their own lives, as compared to 3% of people who have not been bullied and were not involved in sexting. Another alarming study from the U.S. Secret Service and Department of Education reports that 71% of the 41 students who shot others at their schools between 1974 and 2000 had been bullied, cyber or otherwise.[55]

These studies show that electronic aggression is not only pervasive, but its associated effects are increasingly significant. Primary effects include emotional distress, depression, suicide, and loss of interest in learning. Conduct problems including increased risk of substance abuse, truancy, and in-person victimization also occur. Children do not have the coping or cognitive skills to insulate themselves from the undesirable effects of cyber bullying. Hence the victims often respond inappropriately by engaging in conduct that further damages themselves or others.

Confronted with the alarming statistics that students abuse and exploit technology, educators must learn how to address this emergent health and safety threat. Schools have a responsibility to promote an educational environment that is safe and conducive to learning. To protect student victims, bullies, bystanders, and educational institutions, teachers and administrators must remain informed about the legal implications of electronic media use and personal expression. When censorship of student expression occurs, schools bear the burden of showing the correlation between the students' expression and the negative effect on the school environment. Hence, this handbook focuses on the following:

- The legal limits within which schools can sanction and regulate a student's ability to create, post, and access online communications under basic First Amendment law.
- The impact of existing legislative and policy provisions in place or being developed on national and local levels.
- Suggested considerations for structuring a solution to digital indiscretions.

The solutions will be presented using a scoring rubric, referred to in this manual as the school sanctioning MATRIX. This MATRIX provides a useful tool for school administrators to reference when dealing with the disciplinary issues surrounding cyber bullying situations. Further, the MATRIX provides a structured point system for determining disciplinary outcomes by balancing aggravating and mitigating circumstances based on school district policies; on federal, state, and local legislation; and on the intensity, duration, and frequency of student conduct.

Challenges Created by Inappropriate Cyber Expressions

A wide assortment of conduct is encompassed by the broad definition of cyber bullying. As a result, sanctionable inappropriate cyber expressions are often difficult to discern from immature, rude, and obnoxious comments and postings. Additionally, the ability of schools to monitor student expression often competes with the interest of protecting free speech. Even the Supreme Court acknowledges that "there is some uncertainty at the outer boundaries as to when courts should apply school-speech precedents."[56] Furthermore, the measuring stick justifying censorship is subject to localized and regionalized interpretations of Supreme Court decisions predating or not involving the widespread usage of personal computers, cyber technology, or the Internet as a communication medium.

Regulating student speech is not an exact science. This handbook discusses factors that should be considered by school personnel when intervening or regulating on- and off-campus expressive behavior by students. The handbook also provides guidance to educators for restraining high-tech incivility among students.[57] These measures ensure a safe and appropriate learning environment without sacrificing the constitutional rights of children, society, and educational institutions. Court precedents and legal concepts germane to cyber bullying behavior provide practical guidelines and structure for determining if a particular student expression exceeds constitutional protection and thus may be regulated or restricted.

Often debated is the degree to which a school should involve itself in the social, nonacademic aspect of student relationships. Should schools serve as the morality police for our children, monitoring as gatekeepers inappropriate cyber expressions? On one side of the debate, some believe that cyber bullying is just uncivil behavior that should be discouraged but not really controlled or legislated.[58] They believe that reports of cyber incidents are mostly media hyperbole, creating an unnecessary cause for expression control. Children have always made mean comments and shared hateful messages with each other about their peers and authority figures. There was no need then, nor is there now, to create formal policies or practices to control this behavior.

On the other side of the debate are those who support school intervention.[59] Most school administrators and school boards fall on this side of the debate. These individuals claim that cyber expression is different from traditional student-to-student expression. Cyber bullying reaches far beyond the classroom and the schoolyard. In traditional forms of bullying, the perpetrator and the victim are face to face, and the audience is limited to those present at the scene. The victim knows the offender(s). The bullying incident, although it can be sustained over time, is limited by the actual contact between the perpetrator and the victim. The victim can escape the tormentor by retreating to a safe place, such as the home or school.

Cyber bullying is different. Cyber expression affords the tormentor(s) a veil of anonymity. Technology instantly provides 24/7 access to the victim, regardless of whether or not the victim is online. This victimization occurs before an unlimited, Internet-based audience of bystanders and supporters. Participation by perpetrators can grow exponentially, as bystanders access or contribute to the inappropriate cyber expressions. The victim cannot escape the electronic message by walking away, closing a door, or turning off the technology. The hateful message remains in cyber space as a cyber footprint. It lurks until the technology is once again activated or a friend's (bystander's) social networking connection is made. Advocates favoring school regulation cite examples of real-life incidents where cyber comments resulted in serious consequences.[60]

Regardless of one's position on this topic, all agree that schools are not immune from student-on-student emotional, psychological, and physical violence. Society, schools, and courts recognize the seriousness of expressions made by students against others. In fact, school violence is such a grave concern in today's world that a Massachusetts court took judicial notice of the actual and potential violence in public schools.[61] The events at Virginia Tech and the school shootings that occurred during 2008 involving Memphis's Hamilton High School, Louisiana Technical College, and Northern Illinois University confirm the gravity of school violence and the escalation of the incidents.[62]

The initial challenge for K–12 school officials is in differentiating inappropriate and sanctionable online expression from free and protected speech. Court cases provide conflicting messages to school administrators. On the one hand, the courts encourage schools to protect students from expressive harm. The Supreme Court emphatically states that schools do not need to tolerate student speech that is inconsistent with their basic educational mission even though the government could not censor similar speech outside the school. Courts have held that schools may regulate speech that interferes with the schools' work or the rights of other students to be secure and let alone. Student speech that assaults another student on the basis of a core identifying characteristic (race, religion, and sexual orientation) may be sanctioned.[63] Those attacks are harmful to minority students' self esteem and their ability to learn. This, however, is not true for attacks based on gender or for nonspecific emotional harm.

Courts tell school officials that they have an affirmative duty to prevent harm. Not only must schools ameliorate the harmful effects of disruptions, they must also prevent harm from happening in the first place.[64] In fact, in March 2010, the Hudson Area School District in Michigan was ordered to pay $800,000 to a student who claimed the school did not sufficiently protect him from years of bullying.[65] The victim endured the systemic attacks from sixth through ninth grade. The incidents included over 200 occasions of name calling (*queer, faggot, pig, Mr. Clean*) in seventh grade alone. He also endured numerous other attacks, such as shoving him into a school locker, urinating on his clothes, and mocking him in classes. The attacks escalated to a point where the victim was stripped naked and cornered in the locker room, and a junior varsity (JV) baseball teammate rubbed his genitalia in the victim's face. The perpetrator was expelled for the few days that remained in the school year but was permitted to attend the school sport banquet. The victim's parents sued under Title IX of the Elementary and Secondary Education Act (ESEA). The court case concluded that the school did not sufficiently employ techniques to curtail the harassment. The school's methods for dealing with peer-on-peer harassment were repetitious, insufficient, and ineffective in stopping the ongoing abuse. The school's actions amounted to a deliberate indifference to the victim's needs.

Although the school administration engaged in a number of interventions, the court concluded that their actions still showed deliberate indifference to the student's needs. Some of the actions taken by the school included parent-teacher conferences, principal conferences, school counselor conferences, special education reviews, evaluations of the victim by the school psychologist, and multidisciplinary evaluation for special education services, with a subsequent assignment to a resource room teacher per an individualized education program (IEP). The IEP team reassigned the victim to regular ninth-grade education courses. The taunting, name calling, and overt aggressive behaviors continued and escalated. Throughout the ordeal, the school met with the offending students and sanctioned them accordingly. However, each time students were reprimanded, a new perpetrator would begin the cycle of abuse.

Although the school did not turn the proverbial blind eye to the abuse, neither did it adjust its remedies to end the matter. While effective for stopping individual perpetrator violence, repeating the same sanctions over and over did nothing to stop the systemic abuse. The unacceptable reaction given by the JV baseball coach illustrates this point. The coach held an all-team meeting telling the players to tease only "men that could take it."[66] The ease with which such a statement was made indicates a tacit tolerance of the bullying behavior. The subsequent sanctioning of offenders did not offset the de facto tolerance permeating the school's attitude. The school had to not only sanction the offenders but also send a commanding message to all stakeholders that such conduct would not be allowed.

On the other hand, the broad authority to sanction expressions has frequently been found to intrude upon the rights of parents to "direct the rearing of their children."[67] Schools may not sanction students' expression merely because students take offense, they fear gossip, their feelings are hurt, they feel insecure, they missed a few classes, or they or their parents are concerned over the student's reputation. Likewise, a de minimis or unsubstantiated fear that the expression might lead to violence is not sufficient for disciplinary actions. "To allow the school to cast this wide a net and suspend a student simply because another student takes offense to their speech, without any evidence that such speech caused a substantial disruption of the school's activities, runs afoul of the law."[68]

In 2009, a California court found against a Beverly Hills school for suspending an eighth-grade student who posted a video on YouTube stating that another student was a "slut," "spoiled," and "talks about boners."[69] The victim and her mother reported the incident to the school counselor. The victim cried, did not want to go to class, felt humiliated, and had hurt feelings. An investigation was conducted, and the school administration demanded that the perpetrator delete the video from YouTube and her home computer. The school counselor contacted the principal, who discussed with the district director of pupil personnel "whether the school could take disciplinary action against plaintiff [perpetrator] for posting the video on the Internet."[70] The district director then discussed the situation with school attorneys and was advised to issue a two-day suspension to the plaintiff. The California district court sided with the student perpetrator, holding that her free speech rights had been violated and that the suspension was improper.

Many cyber expressions have the potential of causing harm or are hurtful, uncivil, or rude, but not all may be regulated or formally restrained. No precise definition or universally acceptable approach for handling online student postings has been proclaimed. The Supreme Court has yet to decide a case concerning school censorship of student expression specifically involving online postings. Lower courts that have addressed the issue are not all in accord. However, most courts do agree that regardless of whether the speech occurs in the physical world or the virtual world, the First Amendment of the Constitution controls its regulation.

State Remedies

Just as the courts have given schools conflicting and confusing messages, so have many state statutes. Some state statutes and state school codes seek to provide students with greater protection than the Constitution provides. Emerging legislation attempts to restore or protect students' rights to free speech. Connecticut, for example, believes that schools have gone too far in restricting free speech. In support of Connecticut's *Senate Bill 1056*, Patrick Doyle of the American Civil Liberties Union stated,

> But we should also protect the rights of parents to raise their own children, the rights of faculty to uphold free speech without fear of discipline, and the ability of school administrators to run their schools without the threat of litigation based on student speech.[71]
>
> At the end of the school day, parents should have the right to teach values and control their children's behavior. The school's teaching mission should not extend into the home to trump the rights of parents to raise their children.[72]

States such as Connecticut and Nebraska are attempting to provide students with the same guarantees of free speech in school that they have out of school. California has given students the same guarantee, with the exception that students must use proper English.[73] These codified variations make it more difficult for schools to differentiate between actionable and inactionable expression over the Internet and between protected and unprotected speech. Furthermore, the state codes seem at odds with some court cases. The challenge is further complicated by the Internet's omnipresence off and on public school campuses. The dividing line between the schools' disciplinary authority no longer begins or ends at the schoolyard gate. Cyber expression sometimes may be regulated regardless of where it originated. Schools increasingly find themselves in uncharted waters. Administrators are making decisions with seemingly no safe or completely correct answer. The Supreme Court itself admits that "there is some uncertainty at the outer boundaries as to when courts should apply school-speech precedents."[74]

It is the purpose of this handbook to provide easy, understandable, workable, and consistent guidelines with which school personnel can address these challenges. By following the legal standards and using the school sanctioning MATRIX, school officials should be able to reach fair, consistent, and just conclusions for handling incidents of cyber aggression.

Notes

1. Olson, M. (2007, July 9). (2007). *Newsmaker: Net generation comes of age.* CNET News. Retrieved from http://news.cnet.com/Net-generation-comes-of-age/2008-1022_3-6195553.html.

2. Lenhart, A., Madden, M., MacGill, A. R., & Smith, A. (2007). *Teens and social media: The use of social media gains a greater foothold in teen life as they embrace the conversational nature of online media, technology & media use.* Washington, DC: Pew Internet & American Life Project. Retrieved from http://www.pewinternet.org/pdfs/PIP_Teens_Social_Media_Final.pdf.

3. Mueller, S. H. (n.d.). Spamming refers to sending unwanted and unsolicited e-mails in bulk that may obstruct the entire system in an attempt to force the message on people who would not otherwise choose to receive it. Definition retrieved from http://spam.abuse.net/overview/whatisspam.shtml.

4. Lenhart et al., *supra* note 2.

5. National Crime Prevention Council. (n.d.). *National Crime Prevention Council newsroom: Cyberbullying.* Para. 2. Retrieved February 24, 2010, from www.ncpc.org/newsroom/current-campaigns/cyberbullying.

6. Patchin, J. W., & Hinduja, S. (2006). Bullies move beyond the schoolyard: A preliminary look at cyberbullying. *Youth Violence and Juvenile Justice, 4*(2), 148.

7. Kowalski, R. M, Limber, S. P., & Agatston, P. W. (2008). *Cyber bullying: Bullying in the digital age.* Malden, MA: Blackwell.

8. Patchin & Hinduja, *supra* note 6.

9. Li, Q. (2007). New bottle but old wine: A research of cyberbullying in schools. *Computers in Human Behavior, 23,* 1777–1791.

10. Bosworth, K., Espelage, D. L., & Simon, T. R. (1999). Factors associated with bullying behavior in middle school students. *Journal of Early Adolescence, 19*(3), 341–362.

Olweus, D. (1993). *Bullying at school: What we know and what we can do.* Cambridge, MA: Blackwell.

11. *Webster's new millennium dictionary of English* (Preview Ed.). Retrieved October 3, 2010, from http://dictionary.reference.com/browse/flame%20mail?r=14. Also, *Some basic Internet terminology.* Retrieved October 3, 2010, from http://www.docstoc.com/docs/28524096/Some-Basic-Internet-Terminology.

12. Willard, N. (2007, April). *Educator's guide to cyberbullying and cyberthreats.* Center for Safe and Responsible Internet Use. Retrieved from http://www.cyberbully/docs/cbcteducator.pdf.

13. Yitch, J. (n.d.). *Bash and slash boards.* Retrieved June 10, 2010, from http://bashandslash.com/boards/viewforum.php?f=1.

14. Mueller, *supra* note 3.

15. *Direct attacks.* (n.d.). Wired Kids. Retrieved October 3, 2010, from http://www.stopcyberbullying.org/how_it_works/direct_attacks.html#code.

16. *Cyberbullying—online bullying: Dealing with cyber bullies, flame mail, hate mail.* (n.d.) Urban75 Info/FAQs. Retrieved March 24, 2010, from http://urban75.org/info/bullying.html.

17. Willard, *supra* note 12.

18. *Id.*

19. *Id.*

20. Patchin & Hinduja, *supra* note 6.

21. *Id.*

22. *Id.*

23. Willard, *supra* note 12.

24. *Id.*

25. *Poke.* (n.d.). NetLingo. Retrieved April 2, 2010, from http://www.netlingo.com/word/poke.php.

26. Shoemaker-Galloway, J. (2007, June 2). *What is happy slapping? A disturbing and violent form of bullying.* Retrieved March 2, 2010, from http://www.suite101.com/content/happy-slapping-a22723.

27. McGill University Social Equity and Diversity Education Office. (n.d.). *Cyber Bullying.* Retrieved February 27, 2010, from http://www.mcgill.ca/files/equity_diversity/CyberBullyingFactSheetdr2.pdf.

28. Haykowsky, T. (2006). *Star Wars Kid cyberbullying lawsuit offers lessons to school boards.* Para 5. An Education Law Email Alert. Retrieved from http://www.mross.com/law/Publications/Email%20Alerts?contentId=887.

29. Six teenage girls film 'happy slap' attack on cheerleader and then put it on Internet. (2008, April 11). *Mail online.* Retrieved from http://www.dailymail.co.uk/news/article-558895/Six-teenage-girls-film-happy-slap-attack-cheerleader-internet.html#ixzz0graZs9IL.

30. The National Campaign to Prevent Teen and Unplanned Pregnancy. (2008). *Sex and tech: Results of a survey from teens and young adults.* Retrieved from http://www.thenationalcampaign.org/sextech/pdf/sextech_summary.pdf.

31. Virk, J. (2009, December 16). Sexting becoming a fad among teens: Survey. *The Money Times.* Citing Lenhart, A. (2009, December 15). *Teens and sexting.* Pew Internet & American Life Project. Retrieved from http://www.themoneytimes.com/featured/20091216/sexting-becoming-fad-among-teens-survey-id-1094259.html.

32. The National Campaign to Prevent Teen and Unplanned Pregnancy, *supra* note 30.

33. McDermott, K. (2010, February 27). State considers new laws to deal with teen sexting separately from pornography. *Herald-Review.* Retrieved from http://www.herald-review.com/news/local/article_b042ce63-9198-57b0-8c8e-99bd07fc943d.html.

34. *States consider new 'sexting' laws.* (2009, April 17). eSchool News. Retrieved from http://www.eschoolnews.com/2009/04/17/states-consider-new-sexting-laws.

35. McDermott, *supra* note 33.

36. *Bebo review.* (2010). TopTenReviews 2010. Retrieved June 12, 2010, from http://social-networking-websites-review.toptenreviews.com/bebo-review.html.

37. *Top 20 most popular social networking websites.* (n.d.) eBizMBA. Retrieved February 23, 2010, from http://www.ebizmba.com/articles/social-networking-websites.

38. *Id.*

39. *Id.*

40. *Id.*

41. *Id.*

42. *Id.*

43. Ngo, D. (2009, May 29). Yahoo 360 to close on July 13. *CNET News.* Retrieved from http://news.cnet.com/8301-1023_3-10252314-93.html.

44. *Zorpia Notifier 1 specifications.* (n.d.) CNET Download. Retrieved February 27, 2010, from http://download.cnet.com/Zorpia-Notifier/3010-12941_4-10671427.html.

45. Belic, D. (2008, November 28). Netlog social network goes iPhone/iPod touch. *IntoMobile.* Retrieved from http://www.intomobile.com/2008/11/28/netlog-social-network-goes-iphoneipod-touch.html.

46. Fox, J. A., Elliot, D. S., Kerlikowske, R. G., Newman, S. A., & Christeson, W. (2003). *Bullying prevention is crime prevention.* Washington, DC: Fight Crime: Invest in Kids. Retrieved from http://www.pluk.org/Pubs/Bullying2.pdf.

47. *Talking with kids about tough issues: A national survey of parents and kids.* (2001). New York: Nickelodeon; Menlo Park, CA: The Kaiser Family Foundation; and Oakland, CA: Children Now. Retrieved from http://www.kff.org/mediapartnerships/upload/Talking-With-Kids-About-Tough-Issues-A-National-Survey-of-Parents-and-Kids-Chart-Pack-2.pdf.

48. *Electronic aggression: Emerging adolescent health issue.* (2008, August 25). Atlanta, GA: Centers for Disease Control and Prevention. Retrieved from http://www.cdc.gov/Features/ElectronicAggression.

49. Wolpert, S. (2008, October 2). Bullying of teenagers online is common, UCLA psychologists report. *UCLA Newsroom.* Retrieved June 12, 2010, from http://newsroom.ucla.edu/portal/ucla/bullying-of-teenagers-online-is-64265.aspx.

50. *Technology and youth: Protecting your child from electronic aggression. Tip sheet.* (n.d.) Atlanta, GA: Centers for Disease Control. Retrieved June 12, 2010, from http://www.cdc.gov/ncipc/dvp/Electronic_Aggression_Tip_Sheet.pdf.

51. Runk, S. (2006, March). *Fact sheet: Cyberbullying.* New Paltz, NY: New York State Center for School Safety. Retrieved from http://nyscenterforschoolsafety.org/factsheet1.pdf.

52. Shore, K. (n.d.) *Preventing bullying in school: Nine ways to bully-proof your classroom.* New Jersey Education Association. Retrieved June 12, 2010, from http://www.njea.org/page.aspx?a=4097.

53. Patchin, J. W., & Hinduja, S. (2009). *Research summary: Cyberbullying research summary: Cyberbullying and suicide.* Cyberbullying Research Center. Retrieved from http://www.cyberbullying.us/cyberbullying_and_suicide_research_fact_sheet.pdf.

54. *Cyber bullying statistics.* (2009). PureSight Online Child Safety. Retrieved from http://puresight.com/Cyberbullying/cyber-bullying-statistics.html.

55. Vossekuil, B., Fein, R. A., Reddy, M., Borum, R., & Modzeleski, W. (2002, May). *The final report and findings of the Safe School Initiative: Implications*

for the prevention of school attacks in the United States. Washington, DC: U.S. Secret Service & U.S. Department of Education. Retrieved from http://www.secretservice.gov/ntac/ssi_final_report.pdf.

56. Morse v. Frederick, 551 U.S. 393, 401 (2007).

57. Dickerson, D. (2005, Fall). Cyberbullies on campus. *University of Toledo Law Review, 37*(1). Retrieved from http://law.utoledo.edu/students/lawreview/volumes/v37n1/Dickerson.htm.

58. Benfer, A. (2001, July 3). *Cyber slammed: Kids are getting arrested for raunchy online bullying. It's definitely offensive, but is it against the law?* Retrieved from http://dir.salon.com/story/mwt/feature/2001/07/03/cyber_bullies/print.html.

59. Ruthven, F. (2003). Is the true threat the student or the school board? Punishing threatening student expression. *Iowa Law Review, 88,* 931–967.

60. Berson, I. R., Berson, M. J., & Ferron, J. M. (2002). Emerging risks of violence in the digital age: Lessons for educators from an online study of adolescent girls in the United States. *Journal of School Violence, 1*(2), 51–71.

61. Commonwealth v. Milo, 740 N.E. 2d 967 (Mass. 2001).

62. Timeline of school shootings. (2008, February 15). *U.S. News and World Report.* Retrieved from http://www.usnews.com/articles/news/national/2008/02/15/timeline-of-school-shootings.html.

63. Harper v. Poway Unified School District, 445 F.3d 1166 (9th Cir. 2006), *vacated* 549 U.S. 1262 (2007).

64. Lowery v. Euverard, 497 F.3d 584 (6th Cir. 2007), *cert. denied* 2008 U.S. LEXIS 6449 (2008).

65. Sorenson, T. (2010, March 9). Michigan jury finds school violated Title IX, awards student $800,000 for peer harassment. [Northwest Education Law Blog.] Retrieved from http://www.northwesteducationlaw.com/2010/03/articles/harassment/michigan-jury-finds-school-violated-title-ix-awards-student-800000-for-peer-harassment.

66. Patterson v. Hudson Area Schools, 2007 LEXIS 87309, 11 (2007), *reversed, remanded* 2009 LEXIS 25 (6th Cir. Mich. 2009).

67. Reno v. ACLU, 521 U.S. 844, 865 (1997).

68. Eversley, M. (2009, December 14). Students go to court to uphold right to be mean online. *USA Today.* Para. 4. Retrieved June 12, 2010, from http://content.usatoday.com/communities/ondeadline/post/2009/12/students-go-to-court-to-uphold-their-right-to-be-mean-online/1.

69. J.C. v. Beverly Hills Unified School District, 2010 LEXIS 54481, 4 (C.D. Cal. 2010).

70. *Id.* at 5.

71. *Free speech statute would restore student First Amendment rights* (2009, April, 14). Inklings Style. Para 7. Retrieved June 12, 2010, from http://www.inklingsstyle.com/?p=142.

72. *Id.* at Para 12.

73. Cal. Ed. Code, sections 48907 and 48950 (2006).

74. Morse v. Frederick, 551 U.S. 393, 401 (2007).

PART I

Resolving School Cyber Situations*

Students have a right to speak in schools except when they don't.

—Justice Clarence Thomas, concurring in *Morse v. Frederick*

*A related publication concerning sections of this part of the book appears in Myers, J. J., & Carper, G. T. (2008). Cyber bullying: The legal challenge for educators. *West's Education Law Reporter, 238*(1), 1–15.

1

Untangling the Confusion Involving Public School Censorship

The First Amendment provides that "Congress shall make no law . . . abridging the freedom of speech." Public school students do not lose this right when they walk through the schoolyard gates. Students possess freedom of expression when they are in the cafeteria, on the playground, and at school-sponsored events. Freedom of speech includes the right to express opinions even on controversial topics. Although repugnant to society's norms, rude, obnoxious, and sometimes hurtful comments are also allowed by freedom of speech. The dilemma is where the line is between when students have the right to speak and when they do not.

No one believes students automatically possess unlimited First Amendment rights in public schools. But mixed messages are conveyed through court decisions as to what are the appropriate limitations. On the one hand, schools have the authority to dictate limitations on student expression pursuant to "the special characteristics of the school environment."[1] **"Learning is more vital in the classroom than free speech."**[2] Schools are told that they

- Need not "surrender control of the American public school system to public school students."[3]
- Need not tolerate expression that is inconsistent with the fundamental values or educational mission of public schools.[4]
- May limit the free speech rights of students in classrooms, "because effective education depends not only on controlling boisterous conduct, but also on maintaining the focus of the class on the assignment in question."[5]
- May punish expression that promotes illegal drug use.[6]
- Have an "affirmative duty to not only ameliorate the harmful effects of disruptions, but to prevent them from happening in the first place."[7]
- Can restrict on-campus speech that is lewd, vulgar, indecent, or plainly offensive.[8]

On the other hand, school leaders are

- Told students do not "shed their constitutional rights to freedom of speech or expression at the school house gate."[9]
- Told they have limited power to insist on civility outside the schoolhouse doors.[10]
- Obligated to provide substantial justification for limiting free debate. "Undifferentiated fear or apprehension of disturbance" or a "mere desire to avoid the discomfort and unpleasantness that always accompanies an unpopular viewpoint" does not suffice.[11]
- Advised that students generally have the right to express themselves freely off campus on their own time.
- Sometimes financially accountable for inappropriately sanctioning students for bullying.[12]

The comments cited above highlight a common confusion felt by school leaders related to their authority to punish students for the content of their expressions. The confusion is further complicated by the emergence of technology usage by students. The parameters of the schoolyard are no longer clear. What expression occurs on campus and what occurs off campus is often blurred. The Internet has become the "most participatory form of mass speech yet developed,"[13] and students are increasingly accessing it to express themselves.

For the most part, the Internet is a free speech zone that is off limits for restriction. In fact, Congress enacted the Communications

Decency Act (CDA)[14] explicitly to minimize government (and school) interference therein. The goal in passing the CDA was to promote the Internet as an unrestrained forum for diversity of political discourse and an avenue for accessible and available intellectual materials. Unless the Internet expression significantly or substantially intrudes within the schoolyard gate or places the safety of others in jeopardy, it cannot be regulated. Add to that the dearth of recent pure First Amendment student speech cases decided by the Supreme Court, the absolute absence of a Supreme Court case addressing a student Internet speech case, and the conflicting decisions surfacing from the lower courts, it is no wonder the issue is muddled. A cursory review of case law precedent reveals that **school officials are damned if they intervene and damned if they don't!**

School authority to intercede in student expression is governed by legislative enactments, school district regulations, acceptable use policies, and prior court precedents. Legislative enactments include state and federal provisions governing criminal activities, civil matters, and state-specific antibullying laws. Most of the legislation and policies concerning cyber bullying are new, having been enacted within the last several years. Hence the constitutionality and effectiveness of these measures have yet to be proven or established. Yet cyber bullying behavior is on the rise. Schools do not have the luxury of waiting for clear laws, proven policies, or controlling legal authority to develop and surface. As a result, many schools turn to the courts for guidance when conflict arises between a school's authority and a student's constitutional First Amendment rights.

Prior Court Precedent

Existing case law exposes the historical boundaries within which the Constitution allows school authorities to intervene and censor student expression. Prior precedent or court intervention is not the magic mirror to look into to resolve all cyber bullying situations. The decision in a 1968 case describes the limitation thus: "Courts do not and cannot intervene in the resolution of conflicts which arise in the daily operation of school systems and which do not directly and sharply implicate basic constitutional values."[15] Courts do not have expertise in educational matters. Schools do.

What courts can and do is provide prior case law guidance as to appropriate boundaries. These boundaries are limited to actual cases and controversies that have been litigated within the judicial system. Since cyber bullying is a relatively new concept, few cyber bullying cases have reached the courts. Notwithstanding that limitation, prior court decisions are invaluable tools for guiding school administrative actions.

Unprotected Speech

Generally, speech, including student speech, is protected under the First Amendment. Beginning with *Cohen v. California,*[16] where the Supreme Court upheld the right of an adult to wear a jacket proclaiming "Fuck the Draft," First Amendment free speech protection is typically upheld with few exceptions.[17] Obscenity, fighting words, sexting, defamation, and true threats are unprotected exceptions to the free speech rule. However, schools may regulate or ban these expressions only within their narrowly defined parameters as **exceptions to the free speech rule**.

Cyber bullying is not necessarily synonomous with these terms. For example, some cyber bullying incidents may constitute true threats, whereas others may not. To constitute a true threat, a statement must be communicated directly to someone, and it must be interpreted as a "serious expression of an intention to inflict bodily harm upon or take the life of the target."[18] This standard is difficult to meet. As the Supreme Court explained in *Watts v. U.S.,*[19] the true threat category requires more than mere political hyperbole. Watts's comment, "If they ever make me carry a rifle the first man I want to get in my sights is LBJ,"[20] could not be taken seriously as a true threat to injure President Johnson. The statement must cause a reasonable person to feel immediately threatened. Thus, most student cyber expression, like Watts's ranting hyperbole, would fall short of the definition of a true threat.

The test for determining whether an expression is a true threat is very high. It requires an **unequivocal intention to harm** someone. The statement must communicate "a serious expression of an intention to commit an act of unlawful violence to a particular individual or group of individuals."[21] Statements made in jest or as parodies do not qualify as true threats. Similarly, conditional threats or threats of future harm are not true threats. Each of these types of expressions may retain some First Amendment protection.

The distinction between protected speech and true threats is exemplified by the rulings in the following cases. In *Lovell by and through Lovell v. Poway Unified School District*,[22] the court found that the student's statement to her counselor was a true threat. Frustrated by the administrative shuffle in getting her class schedule changed, a tenth-grade student uttered under her breath to her counselor, "If you don't give me this schedule change, I'm going to shoot you!"[23]

The court found this statement to be a true threat, because a reasonable person would interpret this comment as a serious expression of intent to harm or assault. Factored into this reasonable belief of harm is the level of violence pervasive in public schools today. Additionally, the counselor asserted that she felt threatened enough by the statement that she reported it to the assistant principal. Hence it was proper for the school to suspend the girl, as threats of physical violence are not protected speech.

Likewise, a face-to-face statement referencing "pulling a Columbine" was found to be a true threat in a 2008 Pennsylvania case.[24] "In today's society, the term 'Columbine' connotes death as a result of one or more students shooting other students and school staff."[25] The court found that referencing "Columbine" with malice or anger can be viewed at a "minimum as 'fighting words' or a 'true threat' or 'advocating conduct harmful to other students.'"[26]

On the other hand, the *Mahaffey v. Aldrich*[27] case found that a student's statements on a website were not true threats and thus were protected by the First Amendment. The Michigan court ruled that the school could not punish the student for publishing the following statements on a website: "People I wish would die. . . ." "Satan's mission for you this week: stab someone for no reason then set them on fire and throw them off a cliff, watch them suffer and with their last breath, just before every-thing goes black, spit on their face."[28] No true threat existed, because the website did not communicate the statements to anyone else or to any particular student. Further, the website contained a disclaimer indicating that the author did not really wish anyone to die.[29] Hence, no reasonable person would interpret his comments as a serious expression of intent to harm or assault.

A court came to a similar conclusion in a Seattle, Washington, case where a student created an unofficial Internet home page of his high school. The senior student created a mock obituary page that allowed website visitors to vote on who would "die" next—that is, who would be the subject of the next mock obituary. The court found that the student's suspension was improper, because no true threat existed. There was no evidence that the "mock obituaries and voting on the website were intended to threaten anyone, did actually threaten anyone, or manifested any violent tendencies whatsoever."[30]

Internet-based cyber speech rarely meets the true threat definition. It is difficult to establish that an Internet comment reasonably creates an unequivocal intention to immediately harm someone. Courts will not uphold school discipline of student speech simply because "young persons are unpredictable or immature, or because, in general, teenagers are emotionally fragile and may often fight over hurtful comments."[31] To create a genuine case for true threat, the victims must establish that reasonable people would interpret the Internet comments as statements to do immediate harm. Several reported decisions reflect the reluctance of the courts to find Internet speech to be true threats.

In 2002, a Pennsylvania court rejected the claim that a middle school student's website was a true threat, even though the website was devoted to ridiculing the algebra teacher. The student's website contained a graphic of blood dripping from a teacher's head. The teacher's head morphed into an image of Adolf Hitler. Furthermore, the site offered $20 for killing the teacher. The teacher suffered extreme distress after learning of the site. She testified that she "suffered stress, anxiety, loss of appetite, loss of sleep, loss of weight, and a general sense of loss of well being as a result of viewing the website."[32] Further, she suffered headaches, was required to take antianxiety/antidepressant medication, feared leaving her home, and was frightened of mingling with crowds. As a result of these conditions, the teacher was granted medical leave for a year, and three substitute teachers were hired to fill her position.[33] Nevertheless, despite her distress and the disruption it caused to the school district, the court still concluded that the website, taken as a whole, did not "reflect a serious expression of intent to inflict harm."[34]

The website was crude, highly offensive, and a misguided attempt at humor or parody, but it was not a true threat. This conclusion was supported by the fact that the website criticized the math teacher's physique and disposition and utilized South Park cartoon characters, historical figures (Adolf Hitler), and songs.

Similarly, in a 2010 Beverly Hills case, a California court found that a video posting on YouTube calling an eighth-grade classmate "spoiled," a "slut," and "the ugliest piece of shit I've ever seen in my whole life"[35] was not a true threat. The court concluded the statements did not show the requisite level of threat to harm, despite the fact that the video received over 90 hits, the victim required some counseling, was crying, did not want to attend class, was humiliated, and had hurt feelings.

However, a 2010 Studio City, California, case found that hostile Internet banter did constitute a genuine threat of harm. The Studio City court concluded that the posting of death threats and antigay diatribes against a boy was sufficient. In this case, visitors to the website left messages for the victim stating that they "wanted to pound your head in with an ice pick" and posted that the boy was wanted "dead or alive."[36] The court recognized the harm that the antigay messages conveyed to the 15-year-old boy. The visitors' postings sought to destroy the boy's life and threatened to murder him. These statements caused his parents to withdraw him from school and to move out of their Harvard-Westlake community. (Perhaps one of the decisive differences between this case and the 2002 Pennsylvania case was that the Studio City victim was a student as opposed to a teacher. Students who are minors typically receive greater protection from the courts than school personnel.) The results from this recent case may spark other courts to acknowledge true threats of harm from Internet postings. Time will tell whether boundaries are set on Internet conduct.

Protected Speech

Much of student expression that concerns school officials is not governed by the exceptions characterized above. Obscenity, fighting words, defamation, and true threats are relatively easy to deal with. Students who truly engage in those types of expressions can always be sanctioned. As unprotected speech, the expressions may always be censored, regardless of whether they originate on or off campus. Of most concern to school officials is speech that falls within First Amendment protection. These expressions are the most perplexing, because they would be permissible except for the fact that they involve minors and impact the educational setting.

Initially, the Supreme Court resolved student speech rights cases with the understanding that children were entitled to full constitutional rights, with minor adjustments due to the nature of the school environment.[37] In a 1943 case, the Court declared that "Boards of Education . . . have . . . important, delicate, and highly discretionary functions."[38] All of the functions that boards of education perform must be accomplished within the limits of the Bill of Rights. "That they are educating the young for citizenship is reason for scrupulous protection of Constitutional freedoms of the individual, if we are not to strangle the free mind at its source and teach youth to discount important principles of our government as mere platitudes."[39]

Now, however, the Supreme Court has shifted and somewhat retreated from its opinion that students are entitled to strong free speech rights. Today's Supreme Court emphasizes deference to school authorities concerning matters of school administration. The Court touts that those First Amendment rights of public school students "are not automatically coextensive with the rights of adults in other settings"[40] and must be "applied in light of the special characteristics of the school environment."[41] Thus, the Court now recognizes that boards of education hold the "authority to prescribe and control conduct in the schools"[42] and "the determination of what manner of speech in [schools] is inappropriate properly rests with the school board, rather than with the federal courts."[43]

Although the Court has granted educators substantial deference as to what speech is appropriate within the confines of the school environment, the deference is not absolute. Specifically, three categories of speech have been identified that school officials may constitutionally regulate. These categories are

- vulgar, lewd, obscene, and plainly offensive speech;[44]
- school-sponsored speech;[45] and
- speech that falls into neither of these categories.

This third category, by far the most prolifically litigated, includes student speech that substantially and materially disrupts the educational institution, threatens the physical safety of students from actual violence, advocates illegal drug use, or impinges on the rights of other students.

Highlights to Remember

- Students possess freedom to express their opinions even on controversial topics.
- The school's authority to intercede in student expression is governed by court precedents, legislative enactments, district regulations, and acceptable use policies.
- Schools have expertise in educational matters, while courts have expertise concerning appropriate legal boundaries.
- The categories of speech that school officials may constitutionally regulate are narrowly defined and difficult to meet. They include
    - vulgar, lewd, obscene, and plainly offensive speech;
    - school-sponsored speech; and
    - speech that substantially and materially disrupts the educational process, threatens the physical safety of students, or impinges on the rights of other students.

Notes

1. Tinker v. Des Moines Independent Community School District, 393 U.S. 503, 506 (1969).
2. Settle v. Dickson County School Board, 53 F.3d 152, 156 (6th Cir. 1995).
3. Tinker, U.S. 393 at 526 (Black, J., dissenting).
4. Hazelwood School District v. Kuhlmeier, 484 U.S. 260, 267 (1988).
5. Settle, 53 F.3d at 155.
6. Morse, 551 U.S. 393 at 402, 408.
7. Lowery v. Euverard, 497 F.3d 584, 596 (6th Cir. 2007), *cert. denied* 2008 U.S. LEXIS 6449 (2008).
8. Bethel School District No. 403 v. Fraser, 478 U.S. 675, 683 (1986).
9. Tinker v. Des Moines Independent Community School District, 393 U.S. 503, 505 (1969).
10. Layshock v. Hermitage School District, 593 F.3d 249, 256–257 (3d Cir. 2010), *vacated* 2010 U.S. App. LEXIS 7362 (2010).
11. Tinker, U.S. 393 at 508–509.
12. Yap v. Oceanside Union Free School District, 303 F. Supp. 2d 284 (2004).
13. Reno v. ACLU, 521 U.S. 844, 863 (1997).
14. 47 U.S.C. § 230(c)(1) (2000).
15. Epperson v. Arkansas, 393 U.S. 97, 104 (1968).
16. Cohen v. California, 403 U.S. 15 (1971).
17. Papandrea, M.-R. (2008). Student speech rights in the digital age. *Florida Law Review, 60,* 1027, 1046.
18. Mahaffey v. Aldrich, 236 F. Supp. 2d 779, 785 (E.D. Mich. 2002).
19. Watts v. U.S., 394 U.S. 705, 708 (1969).
20. *Id.* at 705.
21. Virginia v. Black, 538 U.S. 343, 360 (2003).
22. Lovell by and through Lovell v. Poway Unified School District, 90 F.3d 367 (9th Cir. 1996).
23. *Id.* at 372.
24. Johnson v. New Brighton Area School District, 2008 LEXIS 72023 (W.D. Pa. 2008).
25. *Id.* at 26.
26. *Id.* at 26–27.
27. Mahaffey v. Aldrich, 236 F. Supp. 2d 779 (2002).
28. *Id.* at 782.
29. *Id.* at 786.
30. Nick Emmett v. Kent School District No. 415, 92 F. Supp. 2d 1088, 1090 (W.D. Wash. 2000).
31. J.C. v. Beverly Hills Unified School District, 2010 LEXIS 54481, 79 (C.D. Cal. 2010).
32. J. S. ex rel. H. S. v. Bethlehem Area School District, 569 Pa. 638, 646 (2002).
33. *Id.*
34. *Id.* at 658.
35. J. C. v. Beverly Hills, 2010 LEXIS 54481 at 4.
36. Williams, C. J. (2010). Court tightens definition of cyber-bullying. *Los Angeles Times*. Para. 5. Retrieved from http://articles.latimes.com2010/mar/18/local/la-me-cyber-speech18-2010mar18.

37. Papandrea, *supra* note 19, at 1038.

38. West Virginia State Board of Education. v. Barnette, 319 U.S. 624, 637 (1943).

39. *Id.* at 637.

40. Bethel School District No. 403 v. Fraser, 478 U.S. 675, 682 (1986).

41. Tinker v. Des Moines Independent Community School District, 393 U.S. 503, 506 (1969).

42. LaVine v. Blaine School District, 257 F.3d 981, 988 (9th Cir. 2001), *cert. denied* 536 U.S. 959 (2002).

43. Fraser, 478 U.S. at 683.

44. *Id.* at 675.

45. Morse v. Frederick, 551 U.S. 393, 430 (2007) (Thomas, J., concurring in the result).

2

Supreme Court Speaks on Student Expression

Substantial Disruption in Schools: The *Tinker* Decision

All discussion on student speech activity must begin by including the relevant principles proclaimed in the seminal Supreme Court case of *Tinker v. Des Moines Independent Community School District*.[1] Mary Beth Tinker and two other students openly violated the Iowa school policy banning armbands in school. The three wore black armbands to protest the Vietnam War and were suspended as punishment. However, the suspension violated the students' First Amendment right to free speech. In their decision, the Court made the now famous statement, **"It can hardly be argued that either students or teachers shed their constitutional rights to freedom of speech or expression at the school house gate."**[2]

Recognizing both the importance of free speech in a free society and the "authority of school officials . . . to prescribe and control conduct in the schools,"[3] the Court created a standard with which to balance the tension between free speech and school policy. The Court held that school officials cannot restrict student expression or punish students merely for expressing their personal views unless the expression substantially and materially disrupts the operation of the school or impinges on the rights of other students.[4] Students have the right to express their opinions, even those disliked by school officials, as long as they do so nondisruptively. The crucial points made in *Tinker* were

1. that students have a limited First Amendment right to protected speech in public school environments,
2. that schools may discipline students for the content of their expression if the expression poses a substantially adverse effect on a school's environment, and
3. that a school may prohibit student expression when it impinges on the rights of other students.

Tinker does not authorize censorship of all expressions of harm related to a school. True threats of violence are always sanctionable. But threats of disruption may be censored only when they forecast material and substantial disruption of the school environment. Passive and nonthreatening expressions are still protected under the First Amendment.

Subsequent U.S. Supreme Court free speech cases expanded the authority of schools to censor the content of student expression. The later cases allow schools to censor the content of student expression

- if it is "vulgar or lewd,"
- if it is reasonably perceived to be inconsistent with the "shared values of a civilized social order,"[5] or
- if the expression negatively espouses any legitimate pedagogical concern.[6]

Many times no showing of a substantial adverse effect on the school's environment is required.

Protecting Students From Inappropriate Speech in Schools: The *Fraser* Decision

In *Bethel School District No. 403 v. Fraser,*[7] for example, school authorities disciplined a high school student after he delivered a speech nominating another student for an elective office. The student's speech was delivered before a school assembly of approximately 600 students. The speech included "an elaborate, graphic and explicit sexual metaphor"[8] describing the nominee. The student used phrases such as "he's firm in his pants" and he's a "man who will go to the very end—even the climax, for each and every one of you."[9] The speaker had previously been warned that using those metaphors was not appropriate and could result in disciplinary measures.

The audience "hooted and yelled"[10] and used gestures graphically simulating the sexual activities referred to in the speech. Some students merely looked "bewildered and embarrassed."[11] Following the assembly, one teacher had to devote class time to discussing the speech. The speaker was suspended from school for violating the *Tinker* rule prohibiting conduct that materially and substantially interfered with the educational process.[12] Holding that the Court must defer to school officials' opinions as to what is necessary to maintain discipline within their institutions, the Court asserted that "schools, as instruments of the state, may determine that the essential lessons of civil, mature conduct cannot be conveyed in a school that tolerates lewd, indecent, or offensive speech and conduct such as that indulged in by this confused boy."[13]

The U.S. Supreme Court supported the school in limiting this expression. The Court held that sexually explicit speech amidst an audience of schoolchildren is not protected by the First Amendment, even absent a material disruption. The Court differentiated this conduct from the nondisruptive, political opinion expressed in *Tinker* and characterized the campaign speech as "vulgar and offensive"[14] but not obscene. The majority decision held that the First Amendment does not protect students who use such offensive language in the classroom or in an assembly. Schools may sanction children who do so.

Speech rights of students are "not automatically co-extensive with the rights of adults in other settings."[15] Children who use an offensive form of expression in a public school will not be given the same latitude permitted to adults; as the ruling in *Fraser* states, "It does not follow . . . that simply because the use of an offensive form of expression may not be prohibited to adults making what the speaker considers a political point, the same latitude must be permitted to children in a public school."[16] Schools have a duty to nurture civility and educate the young for citizenship.[17] Deference will be given to school officials to promote "socially appropriate behavior."[18] To allow such vulgar and lewd comments in an educational setting would be entirely inconsistent with the fundamental values of public school education.[19] Hence schools, per *Fraser,* may restrict nonobscene speech if it is "offensively lewd and indecent."[20]

According to *Fraser,* there is no First Amendment protection for "lewd," "vulgar," "indecent," and "plainly offensive" speech in school.

Fraser permits a school to prohibit words that offend for the same reasons that obscenity offends. Sometimes it is appropriate to limit student speech rights, because schools play an important role in protecting minors from sexually explicit, indecent, or lewd speech.[21] Accordingly, based on this reasoning, *Fraser* censorship "speaks to the form and manner of student speech, not its substance. It addresses the mode of expression, not its content or viewpoint."[22] *Fraser* speaks to the form and manner of student speech, not its substance or viewpoint. Thus, *Fraser* permits censorship of student expression that is "ungrammatical, poorly written, inadequately researched, biased or prejudiced, vulgar or profane, or unsuitable for immature audiences."

Protecting School Pedagogy: The *Hazelwood* Decision

In 1988, the U.S. Supreme Court decided its third free speech case concerning school children. *Hazelwood School District v. Kuhlmeier*[23] discussed the authority of school officials to control student speech and expression that bears the school's official imprimatur (authorization or official approval). The case involved student newspaper authors who wrote stories that described other students' experiences with pregnancy and divorce. The student reporters were required to submit their articles for review prior to publishing. Upon review, the principal rejected the articles for publication. In its holding, the Court created another categorical limitation on a student's free speech rights in the school setting. Schools need not tolerate inappropriate student expression that could "fairly be characterized as part of the school curriculum."[24] In particular, schools need not tolerate student expressions in school-sponsored publications that could reasonably be perceived as inconsistent with the school's pedagogical purposes. No school should be forced to tolerate student expression that promotes irresponsible sex in one of its own publications.

A school newspaper is not a public forum for public expression. A school does not possess the attributes of streets, parks, and other traditional public forums; therefore, school officials may regulate the content of students' newspapers "in any reasonable manner."[25] Additionally, since the school newspaper is not a public forum, no *Tinker* display of a substantial disruption is necessary. In *Tinker*, the Court addressed the "educators' ability to silence a student's personal expression that happens to occur on the school premises."[26] In *Hazelwood,* the Court addressed an entirely different issue, namely, the "educators' authority to supervise school-sponsored publications, theatrical productions, and other expressive activities that students, parents, and members of the public might reasonably perceive to bear the imprimatur of the school."[27] Educators are entitled to exercise greater control over this second form of student expression.[28]

The *Hazelwood* decision crafted an additional, yet narrow, exception to the authority that school administrators have over school-sponsored proceedings. That authority includes control over expressions that can "fairly be characterized as part of the school curriculum."[29] *Hazelwood* allows educators to control school-sponsored proceedings "to assure that participants learn whatever lessons the activity is designed to teach, that readers or listeners are not exposed to material that may be inappropriate for their level of maturity, and that the views of the individual speaker are not erroneously attributed to the school."[30] Thus, *Hazelwood* extends school authority of censorship to matters that may be "reasonably related to legitimate pedagogical concerns."[31]

The outcry from strict First Amendment proponents against the *Hazelwood* decision has resulted in seven states passing student publication policies that limit the ability of school officials to censor school-sponsored materials. The states that have passed this anti-*Hazelwood* legislation are Arkansas, California, Colorado, Iowa, Kansas, Massachusetts, and Oregon.[32] This legislation restores uncensored free speech rights to students. Proponents of these bills seek to return to the original belief that students' First Amendment rights are essential to their preparation for citizenship and should therefore be rarely limited.

Following its *Hazelwood* course of action, the U.S. Supreme Court reexamined student expression in public schools. In 2007, the Court handed down its most recent student school expression case in *Morse v. Frederick.*[33] In this case, a student displayed a 14-foot banner that read "BONG HiTS 4 JESUS" across the street from a school-sponsored event.[34] After the student refused to take down the banner, the principal confiscated it and suspended the student. In an explicitly narrow decision, the U.S. Supreme Court held that "schools may take steps to safeguard those entrusted to their care from speech that can reasonably be regarded as encouraging illegal drug use."[35] Principal Morse was justified in her actions. She had reasonably interpreted the sign as promoting an expression that contributed to the dangers of illegal drug use.[36] Failing to react to the sign "would send a powerful message to students . . . about how serious the school was about the dangers of illegal drug use."[37] The student's claim that his expression could not be monitored due to his position off campus (across the street from the school) was also rejected. The Court found the argument ludicrous and stated, "Frederick cannot stand in the midst of his fellow students, during school hours, at a school-sanctioned activity and claim he is not at school."[38]

Similar to its holding in *Fraser,* the Court's conclusion in *Morse* was that the student's speech was inappropriate as to time, place, and manner. At a school event, a student may not promote illegal drug usage. Hence, the school may censor the student's action without showing a material and substantial disruption to the educational program, as required by *Tinker*. School officials are certainly allowed to balance their authority between educational concerns and students' First Amendment rights. Student expression may be censored or restricted when the school authorities provide a compelling and legitimate pedagogical reason to do so.[39]

Highlights to Remember

- The seminal Supreme Court case *Tinker v. Des Moines Independent Community School District* limited school officials' ability to restrict students' personal expressions.
- Censorship of student expression is permissible when the expression substantially and materially disrupts the operation of the school or impinges on the rights of other students.
- Not *all* threats of disruption or disruptions caused by expression may be censored.
- The First Amendment does not protect students when they use offensive language in the classroom, at a school-sponsored activity, or at an assembly.
- Children at school are not permitted the same latitude of freedom of expression as adults.
- Schools have a responsibility to nurture civility, to educate the young for citizenship, and to promote socially appropriate behaviors.
- The decision in *Bethel School District No. 403 v. Fraser* permits school officials to censor student expression that is ungrammatical, vulgar or profane, or unsuitable for immature audiences.
- *Hazelwood School District v. Kuhlmeier* grants school officials the authority to control student expression that bears the school's official imprimatur.
- Educators are entitled to exercise control over student expression and school-authorized publications, productions, and activities that are characterized as part of the school curriculum.
- A school's authority to censor student expression must be reasonably related to a legitimate pedagogical concern.

Notes

1. Tinker v. Des Moines Independent Community School District, 393 U.S. 503 (1969).
2. *Id.* at 506.
3. *Id.* at 507.
4. *Id.* at 509.
5. Bethel School District No. 403 v. Fraser, 478 U.S. 675, 683 (1986).
6. Hazelwood School District v. Kuhlmeier, 484 U.S. 260, 273 (1988).
7. Fraser, 478 U.S. 675.
8. *Id.* at 677.
9. *Id.* at 687 (Brennan, J., concurring).
10. *Id.* at 678.
11. *Id.*
12. *Id.*
13. *Id.* at 683.
14. *Id.* at 684.
15. Bethel School District No. 403 v. Fraser, 478 U.S. 675, 682 (1986), citing New Jersey v. T.L.O., 469 U.S. 325, 340-342 (1985).
16. Fraser, 478 U.S. 675.
17. West Virginia State Board of Education v. Barnette, 319 U.S. 624, 631 (1943).
18. Fraser, 478 U.S. at 681.
19. *Id.* at 685–686.
20. *Id.* at 685.
21. *Id.* at 684–685.
22. East High Gay/Straight Alliance v. Board of Educ. of Salt Lake City School District, 81 F. Supp. 2d 1166, 1193 (D. Utah 1999).
23. *Id.*
24. *Id.* at 271.
25. *Id.* at 270.
26. Layshock v. Hermitage School District, 593 F.3d 249, 257 (3d Cir. 2010), *vacated.*
27. Saxe v. State College Area School District, 240 F.3d 200, 213 (3d Cir. 2001).
28. *Id.*
29. *Id.*
30. *Id.*
31. *Id.* at 273.
32. Hiestand, M. (2001). *Understanding "anti-Hazelwood" laws.* Arlington, VA: National Scholastic Press Association. Retrieved from http://www.studentpress.org/nspa/trends/~law0101hs.html.
33. Morse v. Frederick, 551 U.S. 393 (2007).
34. *Id.* at 397.
35. *Id.* at 426 (Breyer, J., concurring).
36. *Id.* at 408.
37. *Id.* at 410.
38. *Id.* at 401.
39. Hazelwood School District v. Kuhlmeier, 484 U.S. 260, 273 (1988).

3

The Local Take on Student Expression

The Supreme Court decisions establish the skeletal bones of protection from government censorship in student school speech cases. The Court's decisions establish the lowest limit to which school leaders may restrict student speech rights. The lower court decisions, however, add flesh to the bones. These decisions attempt to define what the high Court's terminology actually implies. For example, how much authority do school administrators possess to discipline students' expression? Supreme Court decisions are scarce, their issues are narrowly defined, and they lack commentary on digital matters. Thus it is not surprising that the lower courts have, to a certain extent, reached different conclusions on student speech rights. The importance of the lower court decisions should not be underestimated. These lower court decisions provide insight allowing school authorities to view how real-world situations have been adjudicated within the bones or framework of Supreme Court mandates.

Rationale for Regulating Student Expression

As previously noted, the Supreme Court has identified three categories of speech that school officials may constitutionally regulate. These are (1) vulgar, lewd, obscene, and plainly offensive speech, which is controlled by *Fraser;* (2) school-sponsored speech, which is controlled by *Hazelwood* (and perhaps *Morse*); and (3) speech that falls into neither of these categories, which is controlled by *Tinker.*

The *Fraser* limitation is premised on the distinction between adults and children. The Supreme Court has acknowledged inherent cognitive and developmental differences between children and adults, justifying a need to treat children differently from adults and to protect their sensibilities.[1] Children are not entitled to the same expressive latitude as adults. School officials may protect minors from exposure to vulgar and offensive language, including cyber generated language. In a K–12 setting "lewd," "vulgar," "indecent," and "plainly offensive" speech offends a child's sensibilities. Hence, the age of the child and the cognitive development level are important considerations in distinguishing appropriate speech from inappropriate speech. Inappropriate speech includes expressions that are ungrammatical, poorly written, biased, vulgar, or unsuitable for immature audiences.

Hazelwood censorship is based on the *special characteristics* of the school environment. Schools need to establish and maintain a level of pedagogical professionalism. It is important that school officials (not the courts) establish the school's educational mission and guide students along that path. To that end, schools may sanction student expression as long as the reasons for the sanction are reasonably related to legitimate pedagogical concerns.

The *Tinker* decision was premised on the Court's strong support of First Amendment principles. School settings constitute a "marketplace for ideas";[2] therefore, they should encourage free debate even of unpopular opinions. Only speech that has the ability to substantially interfere with the actual operation of the school should be censored. The content of the speech is not the controlling factor authorizing censorship. The reaction to the expression, its nexus to school territory, and school functioning are the more relevant inquiries.

In Loco Parentis

Interspersed with these justifications is the often-mentioned perception that schools act in loco parentis; therefore, school officials may respond to situations as if they were the parent of the child concerned. Under the common law, school leaders stood in loco parentis over the students entrusted to their care.[3] School children had the amount of freedom that parents and administrators deemed best.

This authority still exists in private schools, but not necessarily in public institutions.[4] Supreme Court cases from *Tinker* to *Morse* now recognize students' constitutional rights, particularly First Amendment rights.[5] Thus, the perception is no longer valid! Children have their own rights, albeit somewhat different in public schools than elsewhere due to the schools' custodial and tutelary responsibility for children, but still they maintain their own rights.[6]

Parents have not voluntarily delegated their authority to school officials when they send their children to public school. Parents have no choice but to send their children to school.[7] Schools do not take over the parental obligation of rearing children. Thus school administrators are not allowed to censor student speech under all circumstances or at all times. A public school's constitutional authority to restrict student expression comes not from the in loco parentis principle but rather from the special characteristic of the school setting.[8] Schools are dangerous places, and it is the environment itself that requires school administrators to protect children, not the abdication or delegation of authority by the parents. Schools have to protect children on school property from "threatening individuals and situations."[9]

During the school day, "children are in the compulsory custody of state-operated school systems. In that setting the state's power is custodial and tutelary, permitting a degree of supervision and control that could not be exercised over free adults."[10] Within this limited setting, school authorities may maintain order and a proper educational environment. Schools may impose standards of conduct that differ from those approved of by some parents. [11] However, where these standards collide, schools must demonstrate a compelling interest that outweighs the parental liberty interest in raising and nurturing their child.[12]

Highlights to Remember

- Since no Supreme Court decision exists covering cyber student expression, lower court decisions must provide the legal framework.
- The justification for censoring student expression is premised on
  - the inherent cognitive and developmental differences between children and adults, and
  - the special characteristics of the school environment as a dangerous place and as a marketplace for ideas.

(Continued)

(Continued)

- Censorship of student expression is controlled by the reaction to the expression, not its content.
- School leaders no longer stand in loco parentis over the students entrusted to their care. Today's children maintain their own rights.
- A school's authority to restrict student expression comes not from the in loco parentis principle but rather from the characteristics of the school setting.
- School authorities maintain control over a proper educational environment and may impose standards that differ from those approved by some parents.

Notes

1. Bellotti v. Baird, 443 U.S. 622, 635 (1979).
2. Tinker v. Des Moines Independent Community School District, 393 U.S. 503, 512 (1969).
3. Vernonia School District 47J v. Acton, 515 U.S. 646, 654 (1995).
4. *Id.* at 655.
5. *Id.* at 656.
6. *Id.*
7. Morse v. Frederick, 551 U.S. 393, 424 (2007) (Alito, J. concurring).
8. *Id.* at 408 and 424 (Alito, J. concurring).
9. *Id.* at 424 (Alito, J. concurring).
10. Gruenke v. Seip, 225 F.3d 290, 304 (3d Cir. 2000).
11. *Id.* at 305.
12. *Id.*

4

Inappropriate Student Expressions Controlled by *Fraser*

A review of lower court decisions within the categories of speech outlined by the Supreme Court provides schools with further guidance for addressing potential First Amendment situations. The first category, controlled by the *Fraser* decision, authorizes schools to prohibit lewd, offensive, and vulgar expressions. In other words, the classroom rights of students include the right to wear armbands in protest of the Vietnam War, but not the right to wear Cohen's jacket displaying the words, "Fuck the Draft."[1]

Schools are responsible for teaching the "fundamental values of 'habits and manners of civility'"[2] essential to a democratic society. Schools must teach tolerance and encourage debate and discourse among students with divergent political and religious views, including minority and unpopular views. Schools must, as Thomas Jefferson dictated in his *A Manual of Parliamentary Practice,* structure the debates such that the sensibilities of fellow students are not offended and all opinions heard.[3] Schools may prohibit indecent language and language that is highly offensive or highly threatening to others.

Limitations of On-Campus Expressions

The limitation within this category is that the expression must originate on campus. *Fraser* does not apply to off-campus vulgarity or expressions. (Those expressions must meet the *Tinker* substantial disruption test discussed in detail below.) Hence, since a significant portion of cyber bullying is created on home computers, the *Fraser* analysis may not apply. What is important is that the offensive expression is heard by an audience whose sensibilities need protecting. In *Fraser,* a **captive audience** of 600 students heard the vulgar speech during a school assembly.

A recent Ohio case emphasizes this point.[4] Jon Coy was expelled from school for 80 days for violating the school's policy against viewing unauthorized websites from school computers. Jon accessed his home-created website from the school's computer lab. The skateboarding website contained profanity and a "losers" section that depicted a picture of a boy claiming his mother had sexually molested him. The school punished Coy pursuant to *Fraser's* rule against a student's use of vulgar and offensive language. The Ohio court, however, ruled that the mere accessing of an unauthorized website, even one that contains vulgarity, may not be sufficient grounds to sanction a student. To sanction under *Fraser,* the school would need to demonstrate that other students viewed Jon's website. Unlike *Fraser, Coy* involved no captive audience of sensitive students who needed protection.

In order to prevail in punishing Coy, the school would need to meet the *Tinker* standard. It would need to demonstrate how the expression substantially and materially disrupted the operation of the school. The school was unable to meet that standard, as Jon quietly and privately accessed his own website without disrupting or disturbing any other student. Typically, the *Fraser* standard does not give schools automatic authority to sanction offensive expressions created off campus.

A Pennsylvania court came to the same conclusion in a 2005 case involving a ninth grader who posted violent imagery in rap lyrics on his personal website.[5] The school found his songs threatening to other students and expelled him for two years. One line from his rap song titled *Massacre* included the phrase, "So watch what you say about me, I'm everywhere son, And the word of mouth is that I'm carrying guns."[6] The court found that the phrase was not a threat, because the words had to be taken in the context for which they were written. Here, the student was simply engaging in "battle rap," a genre in which rappers try to outdo one another by flexing their lyrical muscles.[7] Battle rap is a verbal exchange including nasty language, but the words do not lead to violence.[8] The "rap songs are 'just rhymes' and are metaphors"[9] containing violent imagery without a violent intent. Further, the lyrics were composed and recorded off campus beyond the authority created under *Fraser.* Thus, the offensive language contained within the rap song could not be regulated by school officials. Although school personnel may regulate student expression while students are within the schoolyard, the "First Amendment limits their authority to play parent when the students are home."[10] Ultimately, the school settled the case for $90,000.

Off-Campus Censorship Requires Substantial Disruption

The off-campus limitation was further reiterated in the *Layshock v. Hermitage School District*[11] case. Using a computer off campus during nonschool hours, a student named Layshock created an unflattering and profane mock profile of his principal on a social networking site. Layshock informed a few of his friends about the website, and as a result, the student body and school officials became aware of it. The student was suspended. The court granted summary judgment in favor of Layshock, asserting that the *Fraser* prohibition against profanity does not apply to speech that occurred within the confines of the student's home, far removed from any school premises. *Fraser* does not give schools authority to punish lewd and profane speech that occurs off campus. The court also analyzed the case under *Tinker* and concluded there was no disruption to the school's operation or educational process. Therefore, the school did not have authority to punish Layshock.

Fraser controls only on-campus vulgarity or expressions before a school audience. School boards have the ultimate authority to determine what manner of speech is inappropriate, but *only* within school settings. Once a school board determines that classroom speech is lewd, offensive, vulgar, or inappropriate for the student audience's hearing, the expression may be prohibited. No further showing is needed. No substantial disruption need occur.

Highlights to Remember

- School officials may prohibit lewd, offensive, and vulgar expressions that originate on campus before a student audience.
- School officials may prohibit language that is offensive or highly threatening to others if the expression meets the *Tinker* substantial disruption test.
- The *Fraser* standard does not give schools automatic authority to sanction offensive expressions created off campus.
- If on-campus vulgar expressions are made before a school audience, school officials may react. No further showing is needed. No substantial disruption need occur.

Notes

1. Cohen v. California, 403 U.S. 15 (1971) at 16; Bethel School District No. 403 v. Fraser, 478 U.S. 675 (1986) at 682, citing Thomas v. Board of Education, Granville Central School District, 607 F.2d 1043, 1057 (2d Cir. 1979).

2. Bethel School District No. 403 v. Fraser, 478 U.S. 675, 681 (1986).

3. Jefferson, T. (1812). *A manual of parliamentary practice: For the use of the Senate of the United States* (2nd ed.). Washington, DC: Joseph Milligan and William Cooper.

4. Coy v. Board of Education of the North Canton City Schools, 2002 U.S. Dist. LEXIS 7713 (N.D. Ohio April 29, 2002).

5. Latour v. Riverside Beaver School District, 2005 LEXIS 35919 (W.D. Pa. 2005).

6. Hip-hop researcher called in rap case. (2005). Music News Blog. Retrieved from http://musicfanlubs.org/blog/2005/08/hiphop_research.html.

7. *Id.*

8. *Id.*

9. Latour, 2005 LEXIS 35919 at 4.

10. *PA high school pays $60,000 to student who was punished for private Internet message.* (2002, November 18). American Civil Liberties Union press release. Retrieved from http://www.aclu.org/technology-and-liberty/pa-high-school-pays-60000-student-who-was-punished-private-internet-message.

11. Layshock v. Hermitage School District, 496 F. Supp. 2d 587 (W.D. Pa. 2007).

5

Antipedagogical Student Expressions Controlled by *Hazelwood*

School officials may censor school-sponsored student expression for valid, content-neutral educational reasons. Valid educational purposes or legitimate pedagogical concerns include

- instilling in students the "fundamental values of 'habits and manners of civility' essential to democratic society";[1]
- teaching students "the boundaries of socially appropriate behavior";[2]
- conveying to students "the essential lessons of civil, mature conduct";[3]
- allowing students to observe first-hand freedom of speech so as to see their constitutional rights at work; and
- censoring the style of expression or expression that may be ungrammatical, poorly worded, biased, and so forth.[4]

Furthermore, school officials may more freely sanction school-sponsored expression than student-initiated expression. In other words, schools officials can regulate speech that bears "the imprimatur of the school."[5] Thus, certain initial questions need to be resolved before schools may regulate student expression.

- Was the expression created as part of a school curriculum or during a school-sponsored activity?
- Was the expression created on a school computer?
- Does the *forum* of the expression signify that the school wishes to affirmatively promote that particular speech?

If the answer to these questions is in the negative, then *Hazelwood's* rules do not apply. *Fraser* or *Tinker* standards should be invoked.

Public Schools Are Not Public Forums

Key to the holding in *Hazelwood* was the determination that public schools are not public forums.[6] Schools are not the equivalent of parks or other open areas where free discourse is allowed. Schools are institutions whose purpose is to facilitate learning. Schools need not tolerate indiscriminate use of their facilities. Speech in schools is reserved for legitimate pedagogical concerns. If school authorities conclude after conducting a *rational basis analysis* that student expression is contrary to valid educational concerns, the school may properly restrict its dissemination.

For example, a junior high school teacher in Tennessee assigned a research paper. Students were allowed to pick their own topics, subject to teacher approval. One student chose as her topic "The Life of Jesus" without approval. When the student completed the assignment, the teacher refused to accept the paper. The student's father sued the school, claiming that his child's free speech rights had been violated. The Sixth Circuit Court of Appeals found in favor of the teacher, ruling that teachers retain control over matters of curriculum and course content.[7] The Supreme Court had established in 1968 that "courts do not and cannot intervene in the resolution of conflicts which arise in the daily operation of school systems and which do not directly and sharply implicate basic constitutional values."[8] Effective education depends on teachers being able to control class conduct and to maintain the focus of the class on particular assignments. "Learning is more vital in the classroom than free speech,"[9] the Sixth Circuit court ascertained. As long as the reasoning for the restriction is related to a valid educational concern, the restriction may stand. In this case, the topic was restricted for rational educational reasons, including the following:

- The student had a strong personal belief in Christianity that would have made it difficult for her to write a dispassionate research paper.
- The student was likely to take any criticisms of the paper too personally or misunderstand them as criticisms of her religious beliefs.
- The topic was one that the student already knew a lot about without doing any significant research. The purpose of the paper was to have the students research a paper on a subject with which they were unfamiliar.

Hence, under *Hazelwood,* it was proper that this teacher be allowed to control school-sponsored expression.

Finite Limitations of School-Sponsored Expression

The Third Circuit Court of Appeals has affirmed that "Hazelwood's permissive 'legitimate pedagogical concern' test governs only when a student's school-sponsored speech could reasonably be viewed as speech of the school itself,"[10] and the Supreme Court has indicated that school "sponsorship" of student speech is not lightly to be presumed.[11] The following Washington case demonstrates this principle.

As a high school junior, Nick Emmett was given a school assignment to write his own obituary. The next year, Emmett, now a senior and captain of the basketball team with a 3.95 GPA, extended this assignment by creating and posting a website from his home outside of school hours. He titled the website an *Unofficial Kentlake High Home Page* and included fake obituaries of his friends and an option to vote on whose obituary he should write next. The website also included a disclaimer stating that the page was not school sponsored and was for entertainment purposes only.

As could be expected, the page became a topic of discussion at the school. The local news station reported that the website was a hit list, even though that term did not appear on the site. Consequently, Emmett was given an emergency expulsion for "intimidation, harassment and disruption to the educational process."[12] The expressions made in the website were not school sponsored despite the fact that the initial inspiration was a class assignment. Further, although the intended audience of the expression was connected to the school, the speech itself was entirely outside of the school's control. Because no one seriously believed the expression was meant to harm anyone and no substantial disruption resulted, neither *Hazelwood* nor *Tinker* applied. Emmett's suspension was improper.

Notwithstanding the argument made by the district that websites can be an early indication of a student's violent inclinations and can spread such inclinations to other like-minded people very quickly,[13] the court still ruled in favor of the student. Citing *Tinker, Fraser,* and *Hazelwood,* the court found that the website was "entirely outside of the school's supervision or control and that there was no evidence that Emmett's page was intended to threaten anyone, did in fact threaten anyone nor did it exhibit any violent tendencies of Emmett."[14] Hence, Emmett could not be punished for off-campus, non–school-sponsored speech "on the basis of undifferentiated fears of possible disturbances or embarrassment to school officials."[15]

The same conclusion was reached when a school handed over authority to the juvenile court system in *A.B. v. State of Indiana.*[16] A. B. had posted several derogatory comments about her principal and his policies on another student's webpage. The webpage was designed to appear as though it had been created by the principal himself (thus it was an impersonation). The juvenile court filed a delinquency petition against A. B., alleging that she had committed acts that if committed by an adult would have been criminal. Her actions constituted "identity deception, a Class C felony, and harassment, a Class B misdemeanor."[17] The juvenile court found A. B. to be delinquent and placed her on probation for nine months. The court reversed the order and vacated the delinquency finding. A. B.'s comments were deemed political speech (criticizing a state actor, the principal of the middle school);[18] therefore, punishment was improper and a violation of the First Amendment.[19]

In the Pennsylvania case of *Killion v. Franklin Regional School District,*[20] school-sponsored speech was defined as "speech that a reasonable observer would view as the school's own speech."[21] In this case, a high school student created and posted a "top ten" hit list from his home computer about his school athletic director's sexual preferences.[22] The list was e-mailed and personally distributed at the school by several students, but not by Killion. Nevertheless, Killion was suspended. Killion's parents took the case to court, and the court ruled in favor of the student. *Hazelwood's* ruling allowing censorship of school-sponsored expression did not apply. Killion was not to blame for the list being brought to school or e-mailed to others. All of his actions were accomplished off campus, thereby giving the school no authority to discipline him. *Tinker* as well provided insufficient rationale to justify restricting student speech, because "the mere desire to avoid 'discomfort' or 'unpleasantness' is not enough."[23]

A similar conclusion limiting a school's authority to reach beyond the schoolhouse gate was reached in New York in *Thomas v. Board of Education.*[24] *Thomas* involved the publication of a satirical underground newspaper. The newspaper, titled *Hard Times,* was modeled after the *National Lampoon,* a publication specializing in sexual satire. *Hard Times* lampooned the school's environment and contained both vulgar and offensive content. The students took great care to create the newspaper on their own time after school hours and to distribute the paper off campus at a store away from the school grounds. They even included a statement in the newspaper disclaiming responsibility for copies found on campus. The students did, however, work on the paper in a classroom, where they occasionally asked a teacher for assistance with grammar. Extra copies of the paper were stored in the classroom closet.

Despite the students' efforts to prevent the publication from being identified as a school-sponsored project, school officials suspended the students for its sexual content.[25] The Second Circuit found the suspension improper. The school lacked the authority to restrict publication because "all but an insignificant amount of relevant activity in this case was deliberately designed to take place beyond the schoolhouse gate."[26] If schools were given authority to regulate off-campus activities such as this, schools would intrude upon the role of parents. "Parents still have their role to play in bringing up their children, and school officials, in such instances, are not empowered to assume the character of *parens patriae.*"[27] School authority and "school-sponsored activity" does not stretch so far as to restrict speech that has a de minimis connection between the speech and the school (unless *Tinker* applies).

Finally, it should be noted that *Thomas* was decided in 1979, both before *Hazelwood* and before the Internet. Territoriality is not necessarily the deciding factor in determining the limit of school authority. It is more useful to decide whether the activity bears the imprimatur of the school. Clearly, this *Hard Times* expressive publication did not. A student is "free to speak his mind when the school day ends."[28]

Even in situations where *Hazelwood* controls, states are still free to grant greater rights to students than would otherwise be protected under the U.S. Constitution. As previously mentioned, eight states, including Massachusetts, have passed anti-*Hazelwood* legislation, thereby extending First Amendment protection to students on school property. In *Pyle v. School Committee of South Hadley,*[29] a Massachusetts court unanimously decided that its state "law protects students' rights to engage in vulgar, non-school sponsored speech as long as it does not cause a disruption at school."[30] Students' freedom of expression includes their right to wear "Co-ed Naked" t-shirts to school. Under existing Massachusetts law, students may express themselves in any manner "as long as the speech is neither disruptive nor school-sponsored."[31] Their law is clear, and since the vulgarity printed on the t-shirts is neither disruptive nor school sponsored, it is allowed.

Highlights to Remember

- School officials may regulate school-sponsored student expression for valid educational purposes, including
  - instilling habits and manners of civility,
  - establishing boundaries of socially appropriate behavior,
  - conveying lessons of mature conduct,
  - teaching proper grammar and styles of expression, and
  - modeling constitutional rights.
- The key to regulating school-sponsored expression is whether the forum of the expression signifies that the school affirmatively promotes that particular speech.
- School sponsorship of student expression is not easily presumed and has finite limitations.
- Schools are not permitted to sanction off-campus activities bearing little nexus to the institution.
- School officials are not empowered to assume the character of *parens patriae* over off-campus activities. In these instances, it is the parents' role to control their child's expressions.
- Generally, students are free to express themselves off campus when the school day ends.

Notes

1. Bethel School District No. 403 v. Fraser, 478 U.S. 675, 681 (1986).
2. *Id.*
3. *Id.* at 683.
4. Hazelwood School District v. Kuhlmeier, 484 U.S. 260, 271 (1988).
5. *Id.* at 270–271.
6. *Id.* at 267.
7. Settle v. Dickson County School Board, 53 F.3d 152, 155 (6th Cir. 1995).
8. Epperson v. Arkansas, 393 U.S. 97, 104 (1968).
9. Settle, 53 F.3d at 156.
10. Saxe v. State College Area School District, 240 F.3d 200, 213–214) (3d Cir. 2001).

11. Rosenberger v. Rector and Visitors of the University of Virginia, 515 U.S. 819, 834–835 (1995).
12. Emmett v. Kent School District No. 415, 92 F. Supp. 2d 1088, 1089 (2000).
13. *Id.* at 1090.
14. *Id.* at 1090.
15. *Id.* At 1090
16. A.B. v. State of Indiana, 863 N.E. 2d 1212 (Ind. Ct. App. 2007).
17. *Id.* at 1215.
18. *Id.* at 1218.
19. *Id.*
20. Killion v. Franklin Regional School District, 136 F. Supp. 2d 446 (W.D. Pa. 2001).
21. *Id.* at 453.
22. *Id.* at 448.
23. Saxe v. State College Area School District, 240 F.3d 200, 212 (3d Cir. 2001).
24. Thomas v. Board of Education of Granville Central School District, 607 F.2d 1043 (2d Cir. 1979).
25. *Id.* at 1047.
26. *Id.* at 1050.
27. *Id.* at 1051.
28. *Id.* at 1052.
29. Pyle v. School Committee of South Hadley, 423 Mass. 283, 667 N.E.2d 869 (1996).
30. *Id.* at 871.
31. *Id.*

6

Disruptive Student Expressions Controlled by *Tinker*

All speech that falls outside of the *Fraser* and *Hazelwood* parameters is controlled by *Tinker*. *Tinker* permits restriction of student speech under two theories: (1) when the expression materially and substantially interferes with the school environment, or (2) when the expression impinges upon the rights of other students. Each of these theories demands that schools provide significant justification for limiting free debate. Undifferentiated fear or apprehension of disturbance would not suffice. Nor would the offensiveness of the student speech justify suppression.[1] If a school administrator seeks to significantly burden free student expression under either test, the administrator must provide substantial justification.

Tinker's Substantial Disruption Test

Two significant issues need to be resolved in order to effectively grapple with cyber bullying situations and the Tinker substantial interference test. The first issue concerns the extent of disruption necessary to allow censorship. Does the expression itself reasonably forecast a substantial likelihood of the disruption of school activities?

How substantial must the disruption actually be to merit sanctions? What types of disruptions are included: administrative, personnel, technological? To what extent is the content of the expression considered? Do violent depictions *sua sponte* (by themselves) generate disruption?

The second issue involves territoriality. Is the speech made physically on or off campus? Does the expression have a sufficient nexus to campus such that school authorities need to regulate it? Does it matter how, when, or why the expression gets to campus? Is it necessary that the expression be accessed or viewed on campus? Is it sufficient that the message was aimed at specific students or school officials? Is it relevant how the speech came to the attention of school personnel? Both issues have been significantly discussed by lower courts and at times with conflicting outcomes.

Tinker requires that before suppressing student speech, the school must be able to reasonably forecast that the expression will cause a substantial disruption of school activities. How do schools meet this burden? Typically, schools are required to significantly evaluate the level of actual disturbance or the risk of potential disturbance before they may act to suppress expression, but not always.

For example, in *Morse,* school administrators were permitted to prohibit student speech that advocated illegal drug use. "Illegal drug use presents a grave and in many ways unique threat to the physical safety of students,"[2] the Court determined, thus, speech that advocates such use may be sanctioned. No showing of disruption or violence was required before school authorities were allowed to intervene. Per Supreme Court Justice Alito's concurring opinion in *Morse,* in some circumstances, schools have the authority to intervene "before speech leads to violence."[3] The magnitude of the interest at stake (prevention of the "serious and palpable" danger that drug abuse presents to the health and well-being of students) may be enough to allow censorship.[4] "Because the already significant harms of drug use are multiplied in a school environment," the Court found "that deterring drug use by schoolchildren is an 'important—indeed, perhaps compelling' interest."[5] Accordingly, school administrators need not evaluate the potential for disruption caused by speech advocating drug use; it is per se unprotected because of the scope of the harm it potentially portends.

The language from *Morse,* permitting censorship of speech that could be reasonably interpreted as advocating the use of illegal drugs, may have opened the door for the censorship of other forms of expression in schools. For example, arguing along a similar vein, the Fifth and Eleventh Circuit Courts of Appeal have permitted school administrators to preemptively punish speech that threatens harmful activity without waiting for the material disruption to occur and without evaluating the potential for disruption typically required under *Tinker*. If expression that advocates drug usage may be categorically restricted because of the special danger inherent to students in school environments, then certainly restriction of student expression "applies equally, if not more strongly, to speech reasonably construed as a threat of school violence."[6]

Specifically, in the Fifth Circuit case of *Ponce v. Socorro Independent School District*,[7] the court found that expression that threatens physical harm might always be restricted. Therein, the judge proclaimed that "speech advocating a harm that is demonstrably grave and that derives that gravity from the 'special danger' to the physical safety of students arising from the school environment is unprotected."[8] The *Ponce* case involved E. P., a student who kept an extended notebook diary written in the first person perspective. The diary described the activities of a pseudo-Nazi group operating on the high school campus. The student author ordered this group "to brutally injure two homosexuals and seven colored" people.[9] E. P. described another incident whereby the group punished another student by setting his house on fire and brutally murdering his dog. The notebook also detailed the group's plan to commit a "Columbine shooting" attack on Montwood High School or a coordinated "shooting at all the [district's] schools at the same time."[10] At several points in the journal, E. P. expressed the feeling that his "anger has the best of [him]" and that "it will get to the point where [he] will no longer have control."[11] He predicted that this outburst would occur on the day that his close school friends graduated.[12]

E. P. shared his notebook and its contents with another student who in turn reported to school authorities that E. P. was writing threats in his diary. E. P. maintained that the notebook was a work of fiction. An assistant principal determined that the writing posed a threat to the safety and security of the students, and he suspended E. P. The court sided with the school against the student and found that since the speech threatened the school or its population, it was unprotected by the First Amendment. Speech that clearly advocates particular harm to the school population may be prohibited by school administrators with little further inquiry. The *Ponce* decision effectively allows a school to ignore or sidestep the protection afforded by *Tinker* whenever a physical threat to student safety exists.

The amount of particular harm that is sufficient to compel courts to forgo the *Tinker* analysis has not been established. Speech advocating an activity presenting marginal harms may not be enough. What is important is the school environment. Schools are dangerous places, and students are required to attend. Therefore, schools may restrict expressions that advocate "a harm that is demonstrably grave and that derives that gravity from the 'special danger' to the physical safety of students arising from the school environment."[13] As Justice Alito's concurring opinion in *Morse* stated,

> Any argument for altering the usual free speech rules in the public schools cannot rest on a theory of delegation but must instead be based on some special characteristic of the school setting. The special characteristic that is relevant in this case is the threat to the physical safety of students. School attendance can expose students to threats to their physical safety that they would not otherwise face. Outside of school, parents can attempt to protect their children in many ways and may take steps to monitor and exercise control over the persons with whom their children associate. Similarly, students may be able to avoid threatening individuals and situations when not in school. During school hours, however, parents are not present to provide protection and guidance, and students' movements and their ability to choose the persons with whom they spend time are severely restricted. Students may be compelled on a daily basis to spend time at close quarters with other students who may do them harm. Experience shows that schools can be places of special danger.[14]

In *Ponce,* the court found that the expressions in the diary demonstrated a grave harm to students based on the character of the school setting and not per se based upon the content of the fiction itself. E. P.'s writings were not sanctionable because they posed a specific threat to any particular student. His writings were sanctionable because a failure to sanction them would send a message to E. P. and others that the school administration would tolerate violent threats against the student body. The school was permitted to punish E. P. because the expressions contained in the notebook created a danger, like *Morse*'s drug expression, that "is far more serious and palpable."[15]

The expressions penned by E. P. espousing massive deaths to the school population as a whole must be considered in light of the school violence frequently occurring within the United States. As instances such as those at Columbine, Virginia Tech, and Northern Illinois University have demonstrated, the school environment makes it possible for a single armed student to cause massive harm to his or her fellow students with little restraint and perhaps even less forewarning. The circuit court thus concluded that

> therefore we find it untenable in the wake of Columbine . . . that any reasonable school official who came into possession of [E. P.'s diary] would not have taken some action based on its violent and disturbing content. . . . School administrators must be permitted to react quickly and decisively to address a threat of physical violence against their students, without worrying that they will have to face years of litigation second-guessing their judgment as to whether the threat posed a real risk of substantial disturbance.[16]

The 11th Circuit followed the same rationale in *Boim v. Fulton County School District*.[17] *Boim* held that school administrators legitimately may censor speech concerning school violence by using *Morse's* reasoning. A student named Rachel wrote a first person narrative fictional piece titled "Dream." After she showed the piece to her friend, a teacher confiscated it. The pertinent part of her writing included the following:

> As I walk to school from my sisters [sic] car my stomach ties itself in nots. [sic] I have nervousness tingling [sic] up and down my spine and my heart races. No one knows what is going to happen. I have the gun hidden in my pocket. . . . Constantly I can feel the gun in my pocket. 3rd period, 4th, 5th then 6th period [sic] my time is coming. I enter the class room my face pale. My stomach has tied itself in ___ knots ___ be able to untie them. Then he starts taking role. Yes, my math teacher. I lothe [sic] him with every bone in my body. Why? I don't know. This is it. I stand up and pull the gun from my pocket. BANG the force blows him back and every one in the class sit [sic] there in shock. BANG he falls to the floor and some one lets out an ear piercing scream. Shaking I put the gun in my pocket and run from the room. By now the school police officer is running after me. Easy I can out run him. . . . Out the doors, almost to the car. I can get away. BANG this time a shot was fired at me. I turn just in time to see the bullet running at me.

> Almost like its [sic] in slow motion. Then, the bell rings, I pick my head off my desk, shake my head and gather up my books off to my next class.[18]

School officials suspended and then expelled Rachel from school, claiming that her rights did not include the right to express these sentiments in light of the special characteristics of the school environment. The court agreed. Referencing numerous examples of school shootings, including two incidents located in close proximity to Rachel's school, the court upheld the expulsion. Schools have an indisputable and absolute power to immediately respond to prevent violence on school property, especially during regular school hours. They need not wait for Rachel to broadly disseminate her expressions or for a substantial disruption to occur. They may act immediately.

> Just as there is no First Amendment right to falsely yell "fire" in a crowded theater,[19] or to knowingly make false comments regarding the possession of an explosive device while on board an aircraft,[20] there also is no First Amendment right allowing a student to knowingly make comments, whether oral or written, that reasonably could be perceived as a threat of school violence, whether general or specific, while on school property during the school day."[21]

The right of students to express themselves depends upon the circumstances and location in which it is done. Thus, in a climate of increasing school violence and heightened vulnerability resulting from the lack of parental protection and the close proximity of students with one another, schools are places of special danger. Some courts have allowed school administrators to intervene to protect the physical safety of the student. But beware, not all expressions of harm justify this intervention. **Only grave harms arising from the particular character of the school setting permit it.**

Tinker established the rule that schools may regulate student expression if the expression "materially and substantially disrupts the work and discipline of the school."[22] No court has held that this standard requires school authorities to wait for a disruption to occur before regulation is permissible.[23] Schools may act when they can "reasonably portend disruption" in light of the totality of the circumstances surrounding the particular situation.[24] In other words, schools may sanction student expression if the school can reasonably forecast that the expression will cause a substantial disruption of school activities. Some courts have gone one step further. These courts hold that school officials have not only an affirmative duty to restore order but also a duty to prevent the disruption from happening at all.[25]

So how do school officials know when it is appropriate to act and when it is not? A number of decisive factors have emerged from case law that assist school authorities in reaching the appropriate conclusion that student expression may **reasonably portend disruption.** These factors include the following:

- Was there an actual and substantial disruption of the educational environment?
- Was the expression itself sufficiently violent or threatening to members of the school that it automatically portends violent disruption?
- What is the record of past disruption?
- Did it truly disrupt administrative practices?
- Was the disciplinary decision based on objective facts or on a subjective emotional reaction to the expression itself?

Was There an Actual and Substantial Disruption of the Educational Environment?

The first factor relates to the degree to which an actual or substantial disruption of the educational environment must occur. Since sanctions are permissible against reasonable threats of future disruption, the real question is how much disruption or threat of future disruption is enough. The answer falls somewhere between de minimis and an actual material disruption. More than mild distractions or disruptions are required, but there is no need for complete chaos. The threat of disturbance must be **fact-intensive.** Yet no magic number of students or classrooms need be disturbed. *Tinker* requires "the existence of facts which might reasonably lead school officials to forecast substantial disruption."[26]

LaVine v. Blaine School District[27] provides a fact-intensive example of an appropriate discipline of a student based upon a projection of substantial disturbance. James LaVine, a high school student, showed a poem he wrote to a teacher. The poem was titled "Last Words" and was perceived by school administrators to indicate a threat to LaVine and other students. The poem included the following phrases:

now I know,
what I must do.
I pulled my gun,
from its case,
and began to load it.
I remember,
thinking at least I won't,
go alone, . . .
As I approached,
the classroom door,
I drew my gun and,
threw open the door,
Bang, Bang, Bang-Bang.
When it all was over,
28 were,
dead,
and all I remember, was not felling,
any remorce . . .
I quickly,
turned and ran,
as the bell rang,
all I could here,
were screams,
screams of friends,
screams of shear horor,
as the students,
found their,
slayen classmates,
2 years have passed,
and now I lay,
29 roses,
down upon,
these stairs,
as now,
I feel,
I may,
strike again.
No tears,
shall be shead,
in sarrow,
for I am,
alone,
and now,
I hope,
I can feel,
remorce,
for what I did,
without a shed,
of tears,
for no tear,
shall fall, from your face,
but from mine,
as I try,
to rest in peace,
Bang![28]

LaVine was expelled from school, and he sued, alleging violation of his First Amendment rights. The court found that the expression created a reasonable belief of a substantial disruption, taking into account that LaVine previously had suicide ideations, had been involved in serious family problems, had broken up with his girlfriend and was accused of stalking her, and had had several disciplinary problems in the past, some involving violence. Additionally, there had been a recent school shooting in a nearby community.

By its actions taken, the school further demonstrated its belief that a substantial disruption was imminent. Out of concern for LaVine and for overall school safety, school officials called his home to see if he planned to attend the homecoming dance scheduled for that evening. Although he did not plan on attending, school security personnel at the dance were warned to be on the lookout for him. Additionally, three school officials contacted the police, a crisis hotline, and eventually a psychiatrist for help. The officials even attempted to have LaVine evaluated by a mental health professional. All of these facts taken together establish that the school had a reasonable belief that LaVine's expression would substantially disrupt the school environment.

Later it was learned that LaVine was not truly a threat to himself or others. He was allowed to return to school and resume his studies.

The information within his school file about the poem—which was necessary and accurate to justify his emergency expulsion at the time he wrote the poem—was no longer accurate. Therefore, the court required that the negative documentation be purged from his permanent files or updated to reflect accurate information.[29]

Tinker established that schools may not sanction based on "a mere desire to avoid the **discomfort and unpleasantness** that always accompanies an unpopular viewpoint."[30] "**Silent, passive expression** of an opinion, unaccompanied by any disorder or disturbance" may also not be sanctioned.[31] Lower courts, like the federal district court for the Central District of California, have explained that the term *substantial disruption* must "equate to something more than the ordinary personality conflicts among middle school students that may leave one student feeling hurt or insecure . . . [or] that [may result in] a handful of students [being] pulled out of class for a few hours at most."[32] **Minor inconveniences** to school authorities do not count. More than a difficult day or an hour of disruption is needed. Making a person **self-conscious** does not count, nor do **hurt feelings**. **General discussions** of potentially sanctionable behavior (such as violence or drug use)—as opposed to specific expressions of intent to perform such behavior—do not count.

In *J.C. v. Beverly Hills,* a California case previously discussed in Chapter 1, the court found that the YouTube posting calling an eighth-grade classmate "spoiled," a "slut," and "the ugliest piece of shit I've ever seen in my whole life"[33] was not a true threat. The posting also did not forecast a **substantial disruption** within the *Tinker* guidelines. The court concluded the statements did not show the requisite level of **threat to harm.** This finding was made despite the fact that the video received over 90 hits and the victim required some counseling, was crying, did not want to attend class, was humiliated, and had hurt feelings. The YouTube posting did not truly disrupt the school's activities, class work, or lessons to be learned. Beverly Hills's school authorities had to (a) address the concerns of an upset student who temporarily refused to attend class, (b) make arrangements for five additional students who missed a portion of one day's classes, and (c) deal with an upset parent. Under the totality of the circumstances, these actions did not rise to the level of a substantial disruption. A counselor spending at most 25 minutes calming a student down and resolving most of the other student issues before the lunch recess did not meet the *Tinker* standard. These tasks fell in line with basic job responsibilities.

The *Tinker* substantial disruption standard was met in *Doninger v. Niehoff.*[34] The principal disqualified Doninger, a high school junior, from running for senior class secretary. Doninger had posted a vulgar and inaccurate message about the cancellation of an upcoming school event on an independently operated, publicly accessible blog. Doninger posted the blog message within hours after she and other student leaders met with the principal to discuss alternative plans to hold the event. The students were specifically instructed that appealing to the public was an inappropriate way to resolve issues between students and administrators. Her blog posting was a clear violation of "school policy of civility and cooperative conflict resolution."[35]

On the blog, she openly encouraged others to contact school officials and to voice their own opinions or outrage about the decision. Her actions resulted in the principal and superintendent receiving numerous e-mails and telephone calls from students and community members complaining about the cancellation. Her action also caused administrators and teachers to miss scheduled activities because of the time it took them to resolve the controversy. Finally, "students were 'all riled up,' a sit-in was threatened . . . and the students who participated in the e-mail were called away from class or other activities . . . because of the need to manage the dispute."[36]

Citing the principles of *Tinker*, the court held that Doninger's blog posting "created a foreseeable risk of substantial disruption to the work and discipline of the school."[37] Consequently, the school's sanction did not violate her First Amendment rights. Three factors were used by the court to come to this conclusion. First, the language ("douchebags" and "piss [them] off more"[38]) used by the student was plainly offensive and potentially disruptive of efforts to resolve the problem. Second, the posting was misleading if not completely inaccurate and was intended to and did solicit or recruit further disruption. Finally, as Doninger held an extracurricular leadership position, which was viewed as a **privilege,** the school could rescind that privilege. The student failed "to comply with the obligations inherent in the activity."[39] The imposed discipline was "reasonably related to the legitimate pedagogical concerns"[40] or the school's mission to "inculcate the habits and manners of civility."[41]

The substantial disruption standard was met in *J.S. v. Bethlehem Area School District,*[42] the Pennsylvania case discussed previously. Although it was not a true threat, the webpage created by an eighth grader titled "Teacher Sux" and including the phrases "Why she should die?," "give me $20.00 to help pay for the hitman," [43] and a picture of the teacher's face morphing into Adolf Hitler did meet the *Tinker* test. The school sufficiently established that the off-campus creation caused a substantial disruption to the institution. The reasons cited by the school inter alia (among other things) included

- the physical and emotional effect on the teacher,
- the fact that she had applied for and received medical leave for a year following the incident,
- the disruption to the school's administration, and
- the demoralizing impact on the entire school community.

The court concluded that the eighth grader's website did in fact cause a substantial disruption of school activities. Additionally, the *Fraser* test was also met after the court found a sufficient nexus between the website created off campus and the school campus, due, in part, to the student accessing the site at school and informing other students of the site. The student's expressions and pictorial displays clearly constituted on-campus, offensive, and vulgar speech before a student audience, thereby justifying punishment.

The *LaVine*, *Doninger*, and *J. S. v. Bethlehem* decisions describe facts that support or forecast a substantial disruption at school. The schools were not merely responding to the everyday student emotional conflicts that occur in educational institutions. In these cases, the school was responding to what it believed to be serious personality conflicts that could have resulted in horrendous consequences. The harm was greater than mere hurt feelings. Serious consequences either did result or could have resulted from the student's unrestricted expression. Thus, the question school officials should ask in these cases is, **is there an actual substantial disruption, or is there a reasonable possibility of a future disruption?** If the answer is affirmative, then school authorities need to articulate specific factual reasons for their belief. The question becomes, is the expression itself sufficiently violent or threatening to members of the school that it automatically portends violent disruption?

As the *Ponce* and *Boim* cases demonstrated, sometimes the expression itself, when made within the confines of a school's environment, is sufficiently violent or threatening to members of the school community such that it automatically portends violent disruption. Those cases involved serious threats against the school's population as a whole or against a particular teacher. General threats or expressions may or may not cause the same result. Disgustingly graphic yet not specifically threatening expressions may sometimes portend disruption. Depending upon the jurisdiction and the timing (post- or pre-Columbine), cases have been decided both ways.

The *Mahaffey v. Aldrich*[44] case is an example of a court finding no substantial disruption based upon the words or the expressions alone. This case involved a "Satan's Mission for You This Week" website wherein Joshua, the student creator, encouraged readers to consider stabbing someone, setting them on fire, and watching them die.[45] Because the school offered **no** evidence that the expressions substantially disrupted the educational process as required under *Tinker*, Joshua's statements were protected by the First Amendment. The website did not cause a disruption. It did **not** contain any specific threats against any particular students. It did **not** bear the imprimatur of the school and was not obscene. It did, however, contain a disclaimer that read, "PS: NOW THAT YOU'VE READ MY WEB PAGE PLEASE DON'T GO KILLING PEOPLE AND STUFF THEN BLAMING IT ON ME. OK?"[46]

In both previously discussed cases, *LaVine* (the case involving the poem, "Last Words") and *J.S. v. Bethlehem* (the case involving the depiction of teacher's face dripping blood and morphing into Hitler), the expressions themselves did not *sua sponte* support the school's censorship. However, other factors buttressed the court's finding of a substantial disruption. Those factors included the student's disciplinary past, his emotional issues, and the teacher's inability to return to school.

Did the Expression Sufficiently Portend Violent Disruption?

Since Columbine, most courts rarely recognize limitations to the authority of schools to punish expression that contains some threatening elements. *Wisniewski v. Board of Education*[47] confirms this statement. The Second Circuit Court of Appeals upheld the suspension of an eighth-grade student named Aaron. He made a crude and threatening icon that depicted a pistol firing a bullet at a person's head. The words "Kill Mr. VanderMolen"[48] (name of Aaron's English teacher) were included. The school's policy was that any threats would be treated as acts of violence. Aaron forwarded his threatening message to schoolmates from his home computer. He did not directly transmit his message to anyone at the school. The school was unaware of the website's content until a student eventually brought it to a teacher's attention. Furthermore, no one seriously viewed the message as an indication of violent intention. Nevertheless, the court found it permissible for the school to punish Aaron for the content of his expression under the *Tinker* substantial disruption test.

No disruption was documented, and no violent intent was established. Significantly, even the police concluded after their investigation that Aaron posed no threat to the English teacher or any school official.[49] The psychologist who evaluated Aaron also concluded that he meant the icon as a joke and had no violent intent. Despite these findings, the one-semester suspension for threatening a teacher—a violation of student handbook regulations—and for creating a disruption in the school environment was affirmed. The school-related disruptions were relatively minor. Mr. VanderMolen commented that the icon scared him and made him nauseous. He was reassigned to another class, minimizing contact with Aaron.[50] It is noteworthy to mention that after serving out his suspension, Aaron returned to school, but the family eventually left town due to peer hostility.

O.Z. v. Board of Trustees of Long Beach Unified School District[51] reached the same result. Over spring break, two seventh graders made a video slideshow about their English teacher. One student posted the video on YouTube. The slideshow was described as

> essentially a dramatization of the murder of Mrs. [teacher's name]. The first slide photo states, "Mrs. [teacher's name] dies." Throughout the slideshow, there are photos of Plaintiff dressed up in a costume, depicting a woman meant to resemble Mrs. [teacher's name]. There is red text on each slide photo that describes the scene. One slide says, "Jelly Donut's knife: haha fat bastard. here i come!" In this same photo, the viewer can see a butcher knife lunging at Mrs. [teacher's name] character from the camera's point of view. The butcher knife is then laid on the fallen victim while the text reads, "hehehe. i'm a shank yoooooooooo!" At the end of the slide show, it reads, "your [sic] dead, BITCH! :D."[52]

Several months went by before school personnel became aware of the video. It was discovered when the teacher conducted an Internet vanity search (a Google search of oneself). After she discovered the video depicting herself, she became ill and was unable to sleep for several nights. She reported it to school authorities. As a result, O. Z. was suspended and transferred to a different school. O. Z. sued the school district and argued that the video was merely a joke and not a true threat. The school argued that the video slideshow reasonably forecast a substantial disruption of school activities. School officials believed that given the violent language and photos contained within the show, a material and substantial disruption of the work and discipline of the school would occur. Further, they argued that the sanction would serve as punishment for O. Z. and as protection for the teacher. The school won the lawsuit even though no on-campus disruption was identified. The court cited *Wisniewski* and *LaVine* as precedents and found without further fanfare that the slideshow created a foreseeable risk of disruption within the school.

What Is the Record of Past Disruption?

One way in which schools can forecast substantial disruptions is to identify examples of past incidents that have arisen out of similar expressions. The most frequently cited example of this is *West v. Derby Unified School District No. 260.*[53] In *West*, the Tenth Circuit Court upheld a student's suspension for drawing a Confederate flag. The drawing violated the school's policy against racial harassment and intimidation. The middle school student, T. W., drew the flag in his math class. Kansas school officials suspended the student for violating its harassment policy. That policy provided, in pertinent part, as follows:

> Students shall not at school, on school property or at school activities wear or have in their possession any written material, either printed or in their own handwriting that is racially divisive or creates ill will or hatred. (Examples: clothing, articles, material, publications or any item that denotes Ku Klux Klan, Aryan Nation–White Supremacy, Black Power, Confederate flags or articles, Neo-Nazi or any other "hate" group. . . . Violations of this policy shall result in disciplinary action by school authorities.[54]

The student sued, claiming that the school officials violated his First Amendment rights. T. W. argued that his display of the Confederate flag could be considered a form of political speech like *Tinker*'s armbands. Political speech by students cannot be lightly sanctioned. School officials need more than **undifferentiated fear or apprehension** of a disturbance to overcome a student's right to freedom of expression.[55] Derby School officials had more. The district had experienced a series of racial incidents or confrontations, some of which were related to the Confederate flag. The incidents included hostile confrontations between students of different races and a fight at a high school football game. Thus, the history of racial tension in the district provided a reasonable backdrop for forecasting disruption caused by a display of the Confederate flag. The school's prohibition was therefore permissible.

The past incidents must clearly demonstrate a well-founded fear of future disruption, not some vague or tenuous connection. A policy enacted in response to racial disturbances will not support sanctioning of all expressions that invoke ill will. Schools must show that the expression itself will likely lead to disruption.

Sypniewski v. Warrant Hills Regional Board of Education[56] provides an example. Warrant Hills School District had experienced pervasive racial disturbances. A white student had come to school with a black face and a rope tied in a noose around his neck. Numerous students came to school dressed in clothing bearing the Confederate flag. Some students "formed a 'gang-like' group known as 'the Hicks,' and observed 'White Power Wednesdays' by wearing Confederate flag clothing."[57] A fight had occurred between a black student and a white student that resulted in one student sustaining a concussion and requiring stitches.[58] As the number of incidents escalated, the district eventually established a policy in line with *West v. Derby*'s. Their policy included racial harassment and "ill will"[59] provisions.

After the policy was enacted, Thomas Sypniewski was suspended for wearing a "redneck Jeff Foxworthy" t-shirt. The school asserted that the word "redneck" was synonymous with the Hicks gang and its racial harassment activities. Therefore, the display of the shirt bearing that term entitled authorities to anticipate disruption at school functions.

It was never entirely established whether Sypniewski was a member of the Hicks group, but he had been observed on numerous occasions wearing Confederate flag paraphernalia. He was sanctioned for violating the dress code, not the racial harassment policy. The school argued that the Foxworthy shirt was potentially disruptive, because the term "redneck" had come to connote racial intolerance.[60] Due to the prevailing "history of racial tension at our school and the possibility that the term 'redneck' would incite some form of violence and at a minimum be offensive and harassing to our minority population,"[61] the school asked Sypniewski to turn the shirt inside out. He refused and was suspended for three days.

The court determined that "in a racially charged environment, a school may prevent racially provocative harassment by name calling."[62] Schools may ban expressions that reflect that sentiment. There was substantial evidence of prior disruption related to the Confederate flag at Warrant Hills. Thus, the school had the authority to prohibit the display of the Confederate flag. The flag is a symbol whose display had had the purpose and effect of provoking disruptions in school.[63] The same could not be said for the redneck t-shirt. The t-shirt logo had no similar disruptive history. In fact, Sypniewski wore the t-shirt several times without incident. He also wore it without disruption or consequence until the last period of his classes. He was sent to the vice principal's office "not because of disruption but because of the view of a security guard that the shirt might violate the dress code or the racial harassment policy."[64] For those reasons, the court found that the banning of the t-shirt bearing the term *redneck* was a violation of the First Amendment. The ill will portended by the t-shirt was insufficient justification to limit free expression.

Similarly, no events occurred at a Texas school that would allow it to ascertain the threat of substantial disruption based on past incidents. In *Chalifoux v. New Caney Independent School District*,[65] a Texas court determined that the school violated students' First Amendment rights by prohibiting devout Catholic students from wearing rosaries. The school prohibited students from wearing rosaries outside their clothing while on school premises, pursuant to the district's ban on "gang-related" apparel. Their school code prohibited the wearing of "gang-related apparel . . . in school or at any school-related function."[66] The prohibited list did not, however, specifically include rosary beads. Because gangs frequently change their identifying symbols, the list of prohibited gang-related items needed to be flexible.

In its analysis of the case, the court found that the wearing of rosaries was **pure speech** to which *Tinker*'s requirement of a "material and substantial interference" applied. Symbolic speech is protectable under the First Amendment. In order to prevail, the school district must show that the students' religious speech caused a substantial disruption of or material interference with school activities. Moreover, even in the school setting, more than mere speculation about disruption and interference is required. "Undifferentiated fear or apprehension of a disturbance is not enough to overcome the right to freedom of expression."[67]

In this case, the district presented evidence that over a span of several months, three students who were gang members wore rosaries on campus as an alleged gang identifier. However, no other on-campus offenses were presented, and the students involved in this case were not members of any criminal gang operating in the school district. "Moreover, during the period they wore the rosaries, they were never approached by gang members because of the rosaries. Nor did [the students'] display of their rosaries cause any disruptions or altercations at New Caney High School."[68] Thus the school district failed to show any evidence of hostility from students at the school or any other threat of interference with school safety. Accordingly, there was insufficient evidence of actual disruptions related to the school or of substantial reasons to anticipate a disruption to justify the infringement on the students' First Amendment rights.[69]

Racial hostility is not the only basis for justifying censorship of student expression. Sexual orientation and sexual preferences have spurred censorship debates as well. In Minnesota, a student was prohibited from wearing a sweatshirt bearing the "words 'Straight Pride' with a symbol of a man and woman holding hands."[70] The principal denied the student's right to express himself after some students claimed they were offended by the message. The school supported its decision by pointing to several fights and an incident of vandalism to a gay student's car on school grounds. In particular, the school cited one incident of gay-bashing that allegedly occurred on school property after a Jesus and Me (JAM) session was held. The school conducted no investigation of the allegation but reported that during the session, students quarreled about Christianity and homosexuality. The school also referenced another incident where a student's car was urinated on and keyed. Again, the school believed that the incident occurred because the student was perceived to be homosexual. The school responded to this second incident by allowing the student to park next to the school building. The principal asserted that these incidents were sufficient to establish a substantial disruption to the educational environment.

The court found otherwise, reiterating the bedrock principle that unless a "school has a reasonable belief that the message will materially and substantially interfere with the work of the school, it **cannot censor a message** [emphasis added] on a shirt merely because other students **find it offensive** [emphasis added]."[71] *Tinker* requires that past incidents of substantial disruptions must have some nexus to the student expression in question. Perhaps with more documentation and investigation into the gay-bashing incident and the details and timing of the car-keying incident, the school could provide evidence of a sufficient nexus. Then the banning of the "Straight Pride" sweatshirt would meet the *Tinker* standard.

The bottom line is that if "a school [can] point to a well-founded expectation of disruption—especially one based on past incidents arising out of similar speech—the restriction may pass constitutional muster."[72] Public school students' First Amendment rights are not forfeited at the schoolhouse door. But student rights "should not interfere with a school administrator's professional observation that certain expressions have led to, and therefore could lead to, an unhealthy and potentially unsafe learning environment for the children they serve."[73]

Did the Expression Disrupt Administrative Practices?

Were school administrators pulled away from their usual tasks to address the situation? Were classes canceled, employees replaced or reassigned, or technicians employed to perform diagnostic tests on school computers or to reset access codes? Did the expression undermine school authority, or was it merely a **personal attack** against a school administrator? These questions pose valid concerns for assessing *Tinker* sanctions.

Routine disruptions in a school setting are normal and do not afford redress. But substantial disruptions or threats of substantial administrative disruptions may warrant student discipline. *Boucher v. School Board of the School District of Greenfield*[74] exemplified how much of a threat of disruption was needed to justify school action. In *Boucher*, a student published an underground school paper containing an article titled "So You Want to Be a Hacker."[75] The article purported to describe how students could hack into the school's computer system. After the article was distributed in school bathrooms, lockers, and the cafeteria, the student author was expelled from school for a year.

District policy prevented misuse of and actual tampering with school computers. The student maintained that expulsion was improper, since his conduct did not technically violate the district's policies regarding student use of its computer resources. In this instance, the student neither misused nor tampered with school computers. Further, he did not disclose restricted access codes nor invade the school's computer system himself. Additionally, no criminal proceedings had been brought against him.

The school, on the other hand, argued that the article "provided instruction to the public and unauthorized persons on how to access the school district computer programs and disclosed restricted access information to the school district's computers."[76] The school's technology specialist testified that the article provided sufficient instruction such that private information (student's grades and disciplinary information) could be viewed and altered. Further, after the paper was distributed, the technology expert had to perform four hours of diagnostic tests on the school computers and change all access codes.[77]

After considering both viewpoints, the court sided with the school and found that although there was no criminal conduct and although the student caused no tangible harm to the school's computer system, the article itself supported an inference of potential future disruption. The article was more than an abstract essay on computers. It served as a "blueprint for the invasion of Greenfield's computer system along with encouragement to do just that. It is a call to action detrimental to the tangible interests of the school."[78] For this reason, it was reasonable for the school to protect its interests from being undermined.

Fear of disruption must be reasonable and sufficiently connected to the school environment to make sanctions permissible. The case of *Bowler v. Town of Hudson*[79] provides an example where the fear of disruption was too attenuated to warrant student discipline. Massachusetts students created a "non–school sponsored club promoting pro-American, pro-conservative dialogue and speech."[80] They advertised the club by placing posters on school walls and bulletin boards. The posters included the address of a website that displayed extremely disturbing imagery, including portrayals of beheadings. School officials required that all posters be removed. They also reworked their school policy to require that all posters be preapproved prior to display. Additionally, no web addresses could be included on any posters. The students claimed that the new policy amounted to unlawful censorship (prior restraint) under the First Amendment.[81]

The school claimed that the content on the website was so disturbing that if viewed by students, it would evoke significant psychological reactions that the school would have to address. The court rejected the school's argument as too speculative. Before the school would experience a substantial disruption, a "predicted parade of horribles would have to occur."[82] "Students would have to (1) view the posters, (2) access the website outside school, (3) discover the links to the disturbing videos, (4) navigate past an express warning, (5) click on the videos, (6) be disturbed, and (7) seek counseling."[83]

Bowler concluded that a **mere possibility** that student counseling or unplanned classroom discussions may be required is not sufficient to predict a substantial interference. But when a school must actively deal with a deluge of calls and e-mails caused by a student's website, the interference is sufficient. *Doninger v. Niehoff*,[84] discussed previously, demonstrated that result. In *Doninger*, the student's actions caused administrators and a teacher to miss scheduled activities because of the time necessary to resolve the controversy.

Did the School Base Its Decision(s) on Facts or on an Emotional Reaction to the Expression?

If the school's reaction to the cyber incident causes the disruption, courts are not so eager to find a substantial disruption.[85] Schools cannot censor expression simply because the content criticizes school administrators or is generally aimed at an institution or a faculty member. The **school bears the onus** to show that it was not simply suppressing "expressions of feelings with which they do not wish to contend."[86] If schools have to devote time, resources, and attention to investigate, correct, or alleviate issues caused by student expression, courts will generally support school sanctions. If student expression undermines the principal's authority or possesses the potential for seriously disrupting educational functioning, schools may immediately respond. **But if it is the school's reaction or response itself that causes the disruption, sanctioning may be improper.**

Both *Chambers v. Babbitt*[87] and *Latour v. Riverside Beaver School District*[88] provide examples where the school's response to the expression caused the disruption, rendering the sanctioning of the student improper. In *Chambers*, the disruption occurred after the enforcement of Principal Babbitt's decision. It was the school's reaction to the punishment for wearing the "Straight Pride" t-shirt that caused the "threatening phone calls, hate mail, and religious protests."[89] The message on the t-shirt did not generate the disruptive activity. Likewise, in *Latour,* the student's battle rap did not cause the disruption at the school, but rather, the disruption, in the form of "students wearing t-shirts stating 'Free Accident' and students talking about Anthony's expulsion,"[90] resulted from his punishment by the school district.

Sanctioning is permissible when the students' expressions cause the disruption. Sanctioning is improper when the reaction by school authorities causes the disruption. Factors that are relevant for consideration include

- the number of students and persons that have viewed the expression,
- the general effect of the expression on school discipline, and
- the school resources that are needed to handle the situation.

It is not necessary to wait for an actual disruption to start. Schools should attempt to prevent the disruption from happening. Several cases illustrate these points.

In *Layshock v. Hermitage School District*,[91] a high school senior created a parody profile, characterizing his high school principal as fat and drunk, and posted it to a social networking site. Layshock created his page using almost no school resources, time, or equipment. The school's environment was not engaged except that a photograph of the principal was taken from the school's website, and the school's site was accessed once from a school computer.

The court characterized the profile as ranging from "nonsensical answers to silly questions . . . to crude juvenile language . . . which appeared to be by and about" the principal.[92] The profile was sent via the social networking site to other students. Eventually most of the student body knew about it. Additionally, three other negative profiles of the same principal were posted to the site by other authors. School administrators tried to disable access to all four profiles but were unable to do so for several days. Approximately 20 students who talked and joked about the profiles were referred for disciplinary action for disrupting their classes. Layshock was suspended for 10 days, placed in the alternative curriculum, banned from school-sponsored events, and prohibited from participating in graduation. Some of these restrictions were eased after Layshock filed suit against the school district.

Ultimately, the court concluded that the First Amendment does not require school officials to wait for a substantial disruption to occur before intervening. Schools may discipline students for inappropriate speech and may preempt problems if they foresee a "specific and significant fear of disruption."[93] However, as mentioned previously herein, a mere desire to avoid discomfort or unpleasantness is not a sufficient basis for discipline. Although Layshock's parody disrupted the day-to-day operations of the school, necessitating time and effort in blocking student access from school computers, the court found no evidence of a substantial disruption. No classes were canceled, no widespread disorder resulted, and no violence ensued. Thus, the school district had violated Layshock's First Amendment rights by the discipline it imposed.

Recently, a Florida court reached the same conclusion, determining that a school could not discipline a student named Evans simply because she created a group criticizing her teacher on a social networking site.[94] The Florida case involved a student who created a group titled "Ms. Sarah Phelps is the worst teacher I've ever met."[95] The group's purpose was to enable students to voice their dislike of the teacher. A few students responded. The school claimed that it had the right to restrict her expression "based upon a concern for the potential of defamation" of a teacher.[96] The court perfunctorily dismissed that argument, claiming that a "mere desire to avoid discomfort or unpleasantness will not suffice. . . . The government may not prohibit student speech based solely upon the emotive impact that its offensive content may have on the listener."[97] Furthermore, the court distinguished this case from *Doninger.* Doninger's blog posting "directly invited an on-campus response in the form of disrupting the school with e-mails and phone calls. Evans, on the other hand, did not attempt to engage other students in any on-campus behavior."[98] Thus, the on-campus connection was de minimis.

"It would be an unseemly and dangerous precedent to allow the state in the guise of school authority to reach into a child's home and control his/her actions there to the same extent that they can control that child when he/she participates in school sponsored activities."[99]

Because her expressions were created at home (off campus), were not accessed from school, and did not portend any disruption at school, Evans could not be sanctioned.

The cases of *Killion v. Franklin Regional School District*[100] and *Beussink v. Woodland R-IV School District*[101] provide similar guidance. In 1998, the U.S. District Court for the Eastern District of Missouri heard *Beussink,* the first student website case. In this case, a high school junior created a website entirely from his home computer and posted it on the Internet. The site was deemed highly critical of the school's administration. Beussink used vulgar language to convey his opinion regarding the teachers, the principal, and the school's own homepage. The student's website invited readers to contact the school principal and communicate their opinions regarding Woodland High School. Additionally, Beussink's homepage contained a hyperlink that allowed readers to immediately "access the school's homepage from Beussink's homepage."[102]

The student himself did not bring, access, or view the link on campus. In fact, another student brought Beussink's website to the school's attention without the student's knowledge. The school administration accessed the site on the school's computer. After the principal viewed the site, Beussink was immediately suspended for 10 days. Because of the school's absenteeism policy, the 10-day suspension would cause Beussink to fail all of his second semester classes and miss graduation.

The district court ordered the school district to refrain from using the 10-day suspension to fail Beussink. Further, the school was restricted from imposing any other sanction against him. The court based its decision on the principal's testimony that the student was disciplined because the principal was "upset by the content of the homepage."[103] **It is not the principal's reaction that counts.** The *Tinker* standard requires evidence of a school disruption, not the emotive impact on the viewer. The school's environment was not disrupted. In this case, the only disruption that occurred was caused by the delivery of the suspension notice in the classroom. Hence, the school district's actions violated Beussink's First Amendment rights.

Per *Tinker,* "Regulation of student speech is generally permissible only when the speech would substantially disrupt or interfere with the work of the school or the rights of other students."[104]As numerous federal and state cases have made clear, official prohibitions of student expression require a specific and significant fear of disruption, not just some remote apprehension of disturbance. The fear must be reasonable and not "an undifferentiated fear of a disturbance."[105] The disturbance must relate to the school's environment and not merely the administration's reaction to it. First Amendment rights may be lesser rights in public schools than elsewhere, but they still exist, and "speech restrictions must rest on some special characteristic of the school setting."[106]

The above-mentioned cases all involved hurtful Internet content aimed generally at a school administrator or a faculty member. However, when the Internet content strikes a professional chord, the opposite conclusion results. For example, in *J.S. et al. v. Blue Mountain School District,*[107] (decided the same day and by the same court as *Layshock),* the court found a substantial disruption had occurred, because the expressions undermined a school administrator's ability to perform his duties.

In *J.S. et al. v. Blue Mountain,* two eighth-grade girls created a fictitious profile on a social networking site from their home computers. The profile appeared to reference the middle school principal, Mr. McGonigle, and a guidance counselor, Mrs. Frain. Although the profile did not specifically identify either by name, school, or location, it did visually portray the principal by his school photo and contained references linking it to the school itself. For example, the profile described the activities of a middle school principal whose interests included, among other things, "being a tight ass; riding the fraintrain; fucking in my office; and hitting on students and their parents."[108] Next to the principal's photo was a quote stating, "fraintrain—it's a slow ride but you'll get there eventually."[109] The students' profile also contained an Internet hyperlink called http://www.myspace.com/kidsrockmybed.[110]

The school district argued that the profile sufficiently disrupted school, because two teachers had to calm their classes while students discussed the profile, and a guidance counselor had to proctor a test so another administrator could witness a meeting among the students, their parents, and the principal. When the girls returned to school following their brief suspension, their lockers had been decorated by other students in celebration. Several other students had to be called out for talking about the event during unstructured classroom work time.

While troubling, these incidents did not amount to a substantial disruption to the middle school sufficient to discipline the students for their speech. The minor inconveniences mentioned above associated with the profile are basic administrative tasks with which school officials typically deal. What differentiates this case from typical administrative tasks and nonsubstantial school disturbances is the profile's potential to cause a substantial disruption to the school's overall functioning and the principal's effectiveness. The girls are sanctionable not because of the particularly disturbing content or the critical personal comments about school administrators on their profile, but rather because the profile portends to demean the principal's ability to perform his job. The court was particularly concerned and persuaded by the profile's blatant allusions to McGonigle engaging in sexual misconduct and "activities clearly inappropriate for a Middle School principal and illegal for any adult."[111]

The profile was freely disseminated within the community and described McGonigle's role and duties as a principal. The profile's purpose was not limited to expressing personal anger against the principal, but rather it established a public forum for "humiliating McGonigle before those who knew him in the context of his role as Middle School principal."[112] To that end, the school did produce evidence sufficiently establishing that the profile undermined the principal's ability to perform his school duties. After the profile was published and the students were punished, respect for school policies and discipline disintegrated, particularly among the eighth graders. Additionally, some district parents expressed **concern about the principal's fitness to continue his job** and "to occupy a position of trust with adolescent children."[113] Therefore the court concluded that as more students and parents learned of the profile, a greater disruption to the learning environment would have resulted. Thus, the preemptive actions by Principal McGonigle in sanctioning the students and removing the profile were proper under *Tinker*. The principal's actions were well founded upon a substantial and reasonable possibility of a future disruption.

Tinker's "Rights of Others" Test

Tinker controls more than situations involving expressions that would substantially disrupt or interfere with the work of the school. *Tinker* also controls and provides guidance over student expression that **invades the rights of others.**[114] "The precise scope of *Tinker*'s 'interference with the rights of others' language is unclear."[115] The Supreme Court has deferred the question whether *Tinker's* "invasion of the rights of others" language extends only to speech capable of triggering tort liability."[116] But in any case, **it is certainly not enough that the speech is merely offensive to some listeners.**

Cases have held that this other *Tinker* test encompassing **invading the rights of others** may stand on its own. This test may allow a sanction if schools can provide factual evidence that the expression sufficiently interferes with another student's rights. Those rights include more than a student's physical right to safety. As a California court stated in *Harper v. Poway Unified School District,* students have a right to be protected "as young as fourteen and fifteen years of age, from degrading acts or expressions that promote injury to the student's physical, emotional or psychological well-being and development which, in turn, adversely impacts the school's mission to educate them."[117]

The Ninth Circuit's decision in *Harper* indicated that there are two prongs under *Tinker:* a substantial interference prong, and an interference with the rights of others prong; either may be used as justification for sanctioning student behavior. The *Harper* court[118] supported the position that a school has the right to prohibit expression simply because it undermines the rights of other students. The case involved prohibiting a student from wearing a t-shirt claiming, "HOMOSEXUALITY IS SHAMEFUL"[119] under the **assumption** that the weaker academic performance of gay students is due to the harassment they receive from their peers.[120] The court claimed that public schools may regulate and "even encourage discussions of tolerance, equality and democracy without being required to provide equal time for students or other speech espousing intolerance, bigotry or hatred."[121] In other words, the Ninth Circuit held that student speech that attacks "particularly vulnerable" students on the grounds of **a core characteristic (namely, race, religion, and sexual orientation)** impinges on the rights of others and could be regulated.[122]

Harper is rarely followed. However, *Harper*'s basic premise is upheld. Speech attacking students on the basis of race, religion, or sexual orientation may be regulated under the "rights of others" standard under *Tinker.*

The potential power of *Harper's* holding was severely criticized and reigned in by the Seventh Circuit Court of Appeals decision, *Nuxoll v. Indian Prairie School District #204,*[123] in 2008. The Seventh Circuit disparaged the *Harper* decision by **requiring more than an assumption that negative expressions would interfere with the rights of others**. Schools need to actually prove that the expressions interfere with the educational environment before censorship will be tolerated.

In the court's opinion in *Nuxoll* [124] Judge Posner rejected the school's argument that it could categorically prohibit derogatory comments concerning race, ethnicity, disability, sexual orientation, and gender.

He pontificated that "people do not have a legal right to prevent criticism of their beliefs or for that matter their way of life."[125] "Tolerance is a civic virtue, but not one practiced by all members of our society toward all others. This may be unfortunate, but it is a reality we must accept in a pluralistic society."[126] Censorship of expression requires a true showing that the expression itself did in fact interfere with students' rights to educational benefits or substantially detracted from their learning environment. **Only behavior or expressions that *actually impinge* on the rights of other students may be censored**.

In *Nuxoll*, the court found the slogan "Be Happy, Not Gay"[127] insufficiently derogatory or demeaning to justify sanctioning. However, the court did not rule out that psychologically harmful speech does exist in the context of race, ethnicity, religion, gender, sexual orientation, or disability. When psychologically harmful speech occurs, restrictions under a *Morse* analysis will be permissible.

Avoiding violence is not the only type of substantial disturbance. From *Morse* and *Fraser*, it is permissible to infer that "if there is reason to think that a particular type of student speech will lead to a decline in students' test scores, an upsurge in truancy, or other symptoms of a sick school—symptoms therefore of substantial disruption—the school can forbid the speech."[128] Because of the special environment within a school setting, school officials have a relationship to students that involves protecting them from harassment. Thus, under proper circumstances, schools may ban offensive comments to maintain a civilized school environment conducive to learning, if the school does so in an even-handed way.[129]

Highlights to Remember

- School officials may regulate student speech when they can reasonably forecast that the expression will cause a substantial disruption to school activities or can document that it already has.
- School officials may sanction without waiting for a material disruption to occur when
  - the expression is demonstrably grave, and the gravity is derived from the special danger to students' physical safety arising from school environment,
  - the threat of disturbance is **fact intensive**, or
  - the disturbance equates to something more than an ordinary conflict occurring at school.
- Factors supporting the existence of or potential for substantial disruption may include
  - A student's disciplinary past.
  - A teacher's inability to return to work.

  - o Past incidents of substantial disruptions that have arisen out of similar expressions.
  - o Disruptions to administrative practices that significantly undermine school authority.
  - o Disruptions that are reasonably and sufficiently connected to the school environment (no mere possibility of disruption).
  - o The number of students or persons effected by the expression.
  - o The general effect of the expression on school discipline.
  - o The amount of school resources used to control or remedy the situation.
- School officials bear the onus of establishing that the expression–not the school's emotive reaction/response–caused the disruption.
- Since the school environment makes it possible for a single, armed student to cause massive harm, school officials must be allowed to decisively address the danger.
- The First Amendment does not permit a student to knowingly express threats of violence on school property during the school day. The heightened vulnerability of the school setting, the lack of parental protection, and the close proximity of students to each other make schools places of special danger.
- Some courts believe that school officials have not only an affirmative duty to restore order but also a duty to prevent disruptions from occurring at all.
- To constitute a substantial disturbance, an expression must be more than merely offensive to some listeners.
- For censorship to be tolerated, **schools cannot assume and must affirmatively prove** that negative expressions interfered with the educational environment.
- Only behavior that actually impinges or interferes with students' rights to educational benefits or substantially detracts from their learning environment may be censored.

Notes

1. Tinker v. Des Moines Independent Community School District, 393 U.S. 503, 508–509 (1969).
2. Morse v. Frederick, 551 U.S. 393, 425 (2007) (Alito, J. concurring).
3. *Id.*
4. *Id.* at 408.
5. *Id.* at 407.
6. Boim v. Fulton County School District, 494 F.3d 978, 984 (2007).
7. Ponce v. Socorro Independent School District, 508 F.3d 765 (5th Cir. 2007).
8. *Id.* at 770.
9. *Id.* at 766.
10. *Id.*
11. *Id.*
12. *Id.*
13. *Id.* at 770.
14. Morse v. Frederick, 551 U.S. 393, 424 (2007) (Alito, J. concurring).

15. Ponce v. Socorro Independent School District, 508 F.3d 765, 771 (5th Cir. 2007).

16. *Id.*

17. Boim v. Fulton County School District, 494 F.3d 978 (2007).

18. *Id.* at 981.

19. Schenck v. United States, 249 U.S. 47, 52 (1919).

20. United States v. Rutherford, 332 F.2d 444, 446 (2d Cir. 1964).

21. Boim, 494 F.3d at 984.

22. Tinker v. Des Moines Independent Community School District, 393 U.S. 503, 513 (1969).

23. Chandler v. McMinnville School District, 978 F.2d 524, 529 (9th Cir. 1992).

24. J.C. v. Beverly Hills Unified School District, 2010 LEXIS 54481, 27 (C.D. Cal. 2010).

25. Lowery v. Euverard, 497 F. 3d 584, 596 (6th Cir. 2007); Karp v. Becken, 477 F.2d 171, 175 (9th Cir. 1973).

26. Karp, 477 F.2d at 175.

27. LaVine v. Blaine School District, 257 F.3d 981 (9th Cir. 2001); *cert. denied,* 536 U.S. 959 (2002).

28. *Id.* at 982–984.

29. *Id.* at 992.

30. Tinker v. Des Moines Independent Community School District, 393 U.S. 503, 509 (1969).

31. *Id.* at 508.

32. J.C. v. Beverly Hills Unified School District, 2010 LEXIS 54481, 70 (C.D. Cal. 2010).

33. *Id.* at 4.

34. Doninger v. Niehoff, 514 F. Supp. 2d 199 (D. Conn. 2007), *affirmed* 527 F. 3d 41, 52 (2d Cir. 2008).

35. Doninger, 527 F.3d at 52.

36. *Id.* at 51.

37. *Id.* at 53.

38. *Id.* at 45.

39. *Id.* at 52.

40. *Id.* at 48.

41. *Id.* at 49.

42. J.S. ex rel. H.S. v. Bethlehem Area School District, 569 Pa. 638 (2002).

43. *Id.* at 644–645.

44. Mahaffey v. Aldrich, 236 F. Supp. 2d 779 (E.D. Mich. 2002).

45. *Id.* at 782.

46. *Id.*

47. Wisniewski v. Board of Education, 494 F.3d 34, 35 (2d Cir. 2007), *cert. denied* 128 S. Ct. 1741 (2008).

48. *Id.* at 36.

49. *Id.*

50. *Id.*

51. O.Z. v. Board of Trustees of Long Beach Unified School District, 2008 LEXIS 110409 (C.D. Cal. 2008).

52. *Id.* at 2–3.

53. West v. Derby Unified School District No. 260, 206 F.3d 1358 (10th Cir. 2000).

54. *Id.* at 1361.

55. *Id.* at 1365.

56. Sypniewski v. Warrant Hills Regional Board of Education, 307 F.3d 243 (3d Cir. 2002), *cert. denied,* 38 U.S. 1033 (2003).

57. Sypniewski, 307 F.3d at 247.

58. *Id.*

59. *Id.* at 261.

60. *Id.* at 255.

61. *Id.* at 251.

62. *Id.* at 264.

63. *Id.* at 254.

64. *Id.*

65. Chalifoux v. New Caney Independent School District, 976 F. Supp. 659 (S.D. Tex. 1997).

66. *Id.* at 663.

67. Tinker v. Des Moines Independent Community School District, 393 U.S. 503, 508 (1969).

68. Chalifoux, 976 F. Supp. at 663.

69. *Id.* at 667.

70. Chambers v. Babbitt, 145 F. Supp. 2d 1068 (D. Minn. 2001).

71. *Id.* at 1071.

72. Saxe v. State College Area School District, 240 F.3d 200, 212 (3d Cir. 2001).

73. Scott v. School Board Of Alachua County, 324 F.3d 1246, 1247 (11th Cir. 2003.).

74. Boucher v. School Board of the School District of Greenfield, 134 F.3d 821 (7th Cir. 1998).

75. *Id.* at 823.

76. *Id.* at 824.

77. *Id.* at 826.

78. *Id.* at 828.

79. Bowler v. Town of Hudson, 514 F. Supp. 2d 168 (D. Mass 2007).

80. *Id.* at 172.

81. *Id.* at 171.

82. *Id.* at 177.

83. *Id.* at 177-178.

84. Doninger v. Niehoff, 514 F. Supp. 2d 199 (2007), *affirmed* 527 F. 3d 41, 52 (2d Cir. 2008).

85. See Layshock v. Hermitage School District, 496 F. Supp. 2d 587 (W.D. Pa. 2007).

86. Tinker v. Des Moines Independent Community School District, 393 U.S. 503, 511 (1969), citing Burnside v. Byars, 363 F. 2d 744, 769 (5th Cir. 1966).

87. Chambers v. Babbitt, 145 F. Supp. 2d 1068 (D. Minn. 2001).

88. Latour v. Riverside Beaver School District, 2005 LEXIS 35919, 7 (W.D. Pa. 2005).

89. Chambers, 145 F. Supp. 2d at 1073.

90. Latour, 2005 LEXIS 35919 at 7.

91. Layshock v. Hermitage School District, 496 F. Supp. 2d 587 (W.D. Pa. 2007).

92. *Id.* at 591.

93. *Id.* at 597.

94. Evans v. Bayer, 684 F. Supp. 2d 1365 (2010).

95. *Id.* at 1367.

96. *Id.* at 1373.

97. *Id.* at 1373, *citing* Layshock v. Hermitage School District, 496 F. Supp. 2d (W.D. Pa. 2007) at 597.

98. *Id.* at 1375.

99. *Id.* at 1372.

100. Killion v. Franklin Regional School District, 136 F. Supp. 2d 446 (W.D. Pa. 2001).

101. Beussink v. Woodland R-IV School District, 30 F. Supp. 2d 1175 (E. D. Mo. 1998).

102. *Id.* at 1177.

103. *Id.* at 1180.

104. Morse v. Frederick, 551 U.S. 393, 437 (2007).

105. *Id.* at 1180. *Cf.* Killion, 136 F. Supp. 2d 446.

106. Tinker v. Des Moines Independent Community School District, 393 U.S. 503, 508 (1969).

107. J.S. et al. v. Blue Mountain School District, 593 F.3d 286 (3d Cir. 2010), *vacated, rehearing en banc* (pending 6/3/2010), 2010 LEXIS 7342 (3d Cir. Apr. 9, 2010).

108. J.S. et al., 593 F.3d at 291.

109. *Id.* at 292.

110. *Id.* at 291.

111. *Id.* at 300.

112. *Id.*

113. *Id.* at 301.

114. Tinker v. Des Moines Independent Community School District, 393 U.S. 503, 506 (1969).

115. Saxe v. State College Area School District, 240 F.3d 200, 217 (3d Cir. 2001.

116. Davis v. United States, 526 U.S. 629, 650 (1999).

117. Harper v. Poway Unified School District, 545 F. Supp. 2d, 1072, 1101 (S.D. Cal. 2008).

118. Harper v. Poway Unified School District, 445 F.3d, 1166 (9th Cir. 2006), *vacated* 549 U.S. 1262 (2007).

119. Harper, 445 F.3d at 1170.

120. *Id.* at 1179.

121. *Id.* at 1185.

122. *Id.* at 1201 (Kozinski, J. dissenting).

123. Nuxoll v. Indian Prairie School District #204, 523 F.3d 668 (7th Cir. 2008).

124. *Id.* at 672.

125. *Id.*

126. Harper, 445 F.3d at 1196 (Kozinski, J. dissenting).

127. Nuxoll, 523 F.3d at 670.

128. *Id.* at 674.

129. *Id.* at 674.

7

School Authority Beyond the Schoolhouse Gate

Due to the technological advances of the Internet and other communication devices, schools need to know how far their authority extends beyond the schoolhouse gate. The determination of whether cyber threats or inappropriate cyber expressions justify regulation usually involves establishing jurisdiction.

- Did the student's expression take place on school grounds or during a school-sanctioned off-campus activity?
- Did the student's expression sufficiently impact school activities to warrant regulation?

The general rule of thumb is that if there is a sufficient geographical nexus to the campus, it is more likely that inappropriate activity may properly be monitored by school officials.

The *Morse* decision, expanding *Fraser's* protection from a "lewd," "vulgar," "indecent," and "plainly offensive" speech analysis to a potential harm analysis, supports this interpretation. *Morse* upheld the school's suspension of a student for displaying a banner that advocated illegal drug use. By justifying this restriction because of the concern that "drug abuse can cause severe and permanent damage to the health and well-being of young people,"[1] the Court effectively opened the door for restrictions advocating other potential injuries to students. In fact, that is precisely what has occurred. The school violence cases (*Ponce* and *Boim*) and the psychological harm cases (*Harper* and *Nuxoll*) demonstrate this result. Each of those cases involved off-campus expressions that caused or reasonably threatened to cause a substantial disruption of or material interference with school activities. Additionally, in each case, the court found no need to "satisfy any geographical technicality in order to be regulated pursuant to *Tinker*."[2]

Territoriality is not the final word in determining the limit of a school administrator's authority, but it does offer some guidance. A review of most lower court cases supports the premise that a *Fraser* finding alone will allow for student speech suppression, as long as the expression occurred on campus or the student accessed or brought the speech to campus. *J.S. ex rel. H.S. v. Bethlehem Area School District*[3] serves as an example. Although created off campus, the "Teacher Sux" website was accessed and shown to students on campus; therefore, the student was rightfully subjected to sanctions.

In comparison, in *Porter v. Ascension Parish School Board,*[4] the court found that an off-campus-created violent message that made its way on campus could not be regulated. In that case a student, Adam, was expelled when his younger brother unwittingly took Adam's drawing to school. Adam's drawing depicted "the school under a state of siege by a gasoline tanker truck, missile launcher, helicopter, and various armed persons."[5] Adam had made the drawing at home two years earlier and stored it in his bedroom closet. His younger brother found the drawing at some point and then brought it to school. When the bus driver saw Adam's drawing, she contacted the school authorities, and disciplinary action ensued. The court concluded that because the student's expression had an insufficient nexus to campus, it could not be regulated. Adam himself did not bring the drawing to school, he did not share it with anyone, and he did not target or create it with the desire that it reach a school- or student-based audience. In fact, he created it privately and stored it for two years in the privacy of his bedroom closet.

The concept of territoriality is useful as a beginning point for analysis. If the expression was created on campus, regulation is probably permissible if it meets one of the delineated student speech regulations proscribed by the Supreme Court in *Tinker, Fraser, Hazelwood,* or *Morse*. School officials' authority over off-campus expression is much more limited. School officials generally have no jurisdiction over off-campus student expressions. Students have the right to freely express themselves when on their own, off-campus time. Those expressions are a matter for parental control, not school discipline. Parents should address the dangers of Internet offerings and proper online, off-campus communications.

The difficult and more troubling question concerns expressions that are created off campus but make their way on campus. The Internet and technology often assist in bringing off-campus expressions on campus. How are these situations to be handled? As the court recently elucidated in *O.Z. v. Board of Trustees*, "The fact that [the student's] creation and transmission of the slide show occurred away from school property does not necessarily insulate her from school discipline. Courts have recognized that off-campus conduct can create a foreseeable risk of substantial disruption within a school."[6] Hence, geographic boundaries generally carry little weight in the student speech analysis. What does matter is whether the off-campus expression is specifically **aimed at or targeting the school or school officials.** If there is a reasonably foreseeable risk that the expression will reach the attention of school authorities, schools may apply First Amendment standards. Expressions created off campus may be sanctioned when a school is targeted for violence, when its administrative capabilities are threatened, or when its officials are compromised in their ability to perform their tasks. Examples of each of these categories of offensive, off-campus, censorable expressions follow.

Targets for Violence

In *Wisniewski v. Board of Education,*[7] discussed previously, the Second Circuit Court upheld the school's suspension of a student under the theory that there was a reasonable and foreseeable risk that an off-campus cyber expression suggesting violence would reach school authorities. The case facts included the student e-mailing 15 of his classmates an icon depicting a pistol firing a bullet at a person's head. The message also referenced killing his English teacher, Mr. VanderMolen. Although the student meant the message as a joke and did not bring the message on campus, the school was allowed to suspend the student for one semester. The court found that because the school had to investigate the incident by interviewing students and replacing the teacher who was the subject of the attack, the school satisfied the *Tinker* test. The school adequately demonstrated that a substantial disruption to the school environment had occurred.

Likewise, in *J.S. ex rel. H.S. v. Bethlehem Area School District*[8] and *LaVine v. Blaine School District*,[9] the courts found the substantial disruption standard was met when students created off-campus expressions threatening violence. The Bethlehem, Pennsylvania, case involved a website titled "Teacher Sux." This website solicited funds to help pay for a hitman. The *LaVine* case involved a poem titled "Last Words," wherein the student's expression depicted the shooting of his fellow classmates. In both instances, school officials sufficiently established that the off-campus creations caused a substantial disruption to the institution.

Two recent cases decided post-*Morse*, in essence, abandoned the *Tinker* substantial disruption requirement when the student's speech threatened school safety. Although neither were Internet-based cases, *Boim* and *Ponce* permitted school authorities to sanction students whose speech gravely threatened violence to the school's population. *Boim* involved a student's dream of killing her math teacher. Her offensive speech was contained in a private notebook that was confiscated by school authorities. In *Ponce*, a student created a diary wherein he described the activities of a pseudo-Nazi group plotting to carry out Columbine-like attacks on his high school. In both cases, no *Tinker* showing of disruption was required.

Administrative Threats

Off-campus activities that **genuinely threaten the functioning of schools** are clearly sanctionable. Two outstanding examples supporting this judgment are *Doninger v. Niehoff*[10] and *Boucher v. School Board.*[11] *Boucher*, although not an Internet case, demonstrates that off-campus expression that disrupts school administrative functioning may be regulated. *Boucher* involved the distribution of an unofficial newspaper that advocated hacking into a school's computers. Although the student himself neither hacked into the school's computer system nor brought the publication onto campus, school officials were allowed to punish him. He created a blueprint that encouraged or enabled others to disrupt the educational system.

Likewise in *Doninger*[12], the student's public website encouraged others to contact the school to complain about the district's decision to postpone a musical event. School officials had to devote substantial time and resources responding and reacting to her criticisms. Thus, it was proper for the school to disqualify the student from participating in extracurricular events and from running for class secretary during her senior year.

Not every off-campus activity rises to the level of disrupting school functioning. In *J.C. v. Beverly Hills Unified School District,*[13] the court limited censorship to only those off-campus expressions that cause a substantial disruption to school's activities. The student's YouTube postings, although offensive and upsetting to a student, did not truly disrupt the school's activities, the class work, or the lessons to be learned.

Compromised Ability to Perform Official Tasks

Schools may sanction expressions that compromise officials' ability to perform their duties. As the Pennsylvania court held in *J.S. ex rel. H.S. v. Bethlehem Area School District,*[14] a school may sanction a student for a website the student creates off campus. J. S. was properly sanctioned for his website called "Teacher Sux." A sufficient nexus was established, because J. S. had accessed the website during class and informed other students about it. Members of the faculty also accessed the website at school. In addition, school officials were the subjects of the website. In light of these facts, "it was inevitable that the contents of the website would pass from students to teachers."[15]

A 2008 case involving a student who created a fake personal profile about his principal on a social networking website confirms a school's authority to regulate off-campus websites that undermine school authority. In *J.S. et al. v. Blue Mountain School District,*[16] the court upheld the school's suspension of a student. Interestingly, the court did not uphold the suspension under the theory that there was a sufficient connection between the website at issue and the school campus, or because the student accessed the website at school seeking to disrupt activities. In fact, a paper copy of the website's content reached the school only because another student provided the principal with a copy of it. The *J.S.* court upheld the suspension by invoking *Tinker's* impinging on the **rights of others** prong. Using the rights of others theory, the court held that the student did not have a First Amendment right to post a parody profile of his school principal on a social networking website. The decision explained that the profile "affected [the principal]'s rights" because "as principal of a school, it could be very damaging to have a profile on the Internet indicating that he engages in inappropriate sexual behaviors."[17]

A court in Washington made a similar finding in *Requa v. Kent School District No. 415.*[18] In that case, a student surreptitiously took motion picture footage of his teacher during class. The student and two of his friends edited the footage, added graphics and a musical soundtrack, and posted the results on YouTube. The completed product included commentary on the teacher's hygiene and organizational habits. The video also featured footage of a student standing behind the teacher making faces, putting two fingers up at the back of her head, and making pelvic thrusts in her general direction. Additionally, in a section preceded by a graphic announcing "Caution Booty Ahead," there were several shots of the teacher's buttocks as she walked away from the videographer and as she bent over. The music accompanying this segment was a song called "Ms. New Booty."[19]

The student admitted to posting the link from his own personal webpage during the summer recess, but he denied that the link disrupted the educational process. Again, the link was not exposed until the following February, when a local news channel discovered the video while investigating a story about YouTube student postings critical of high school teachers.[20] Also the school's computers are specifically configured to prevent accessing websites such as YouTube and social networking sites on campus.

The court found the spirit of the video to be "lewd and offensive and devoid of political or critical content."[21] "Those portions of the video featuring (1) footage of a student making 'rabbit ears' and a pelvic thrust behind her back, and (2) footage of her buttocks accompanied by graphics stating 'Caution Booty Ahead' and a 'booty' rap song"[22] clearly interfere with or compromise her role as an authority figure. The video constitutes a material and substantial disruption to the work and discipline of the school. In conclusion, the court found as follows:

> The school district is not required to establish that an actual educational discourse was disrupted by the student's activity. The **"work and discipline of the school" includes the maintenance of a civil and respectful atmosphere toward teachers and students alike** [emphasis added]—demeaning, derogatory, sexually suggestive behavior toward an unsuspecting teacher in a classroom poses a disruption of that mission whenever it occurs.[23]

Schools do not have unlimited authority to punish students for lewd and offensive speech against school officials posted on the Internet.

Not all cyber aggression toward teachers or school personnel meets the *Tinker* standard. The First Amendment protected a student's rights when he published a top ten list commenting on the school's athletic director's appearance and the size of his genitals.[24] The school was not entitled to suspend the student, because his off-campus activity did not result in any disruption to the school, and it was unreasonable to believe that it would result in a substantial disruption. The student composed and distributed his top ten list entirely from his home computer. The list made its way to school only after someone else reformatted the student's original e-mail and distributed it on school grounds.

The list circulated for more than a week before school officials took action. During that week, there were minimal complaints, and no teachers reported being incapable of teaching or controlling student behavior. No one was threatened; however, some were upset. Admittedly, the list was rude, abusive, and demeaning. However, "disliking or being upset by the content of a student's speech is not an acceptable justification for limiting student speech under *Tinker*."[25] Furthermore, the list did not realistically "impair the administration's ability to appropriately discipline the students."[26] The court refused to accept, without more evidence, "that the childish and boorish antics of a minor could impair the administrators' abilities to discipline students and maintain control" or that "the future course of the administration of discipline . . . [will] dissolve, willy-nilly, in the face of the digital posturing of this splenetic, bad-mannered little boy."[27]

In *M.K. v. Three Rivers Local School District*, No. 1:07CV1011,[28] an Ohio court made similar comments in support of students' First Amendment claims. Therein the court rejected the school's claim that a student's parody of a teacher's profile on a social networking website caused a substantial disruption. The court refused to believe that such a boorish antic could sufficiently undermine a school's authority, despite the school's assertion that the profile decreased morale among the teachers, caused the loss of valuable administrative time, and increased anxiety among personnel. These decisions suggest that school officials need to be more thick-skinned. School officials must educate children in proper netiquette, not harshly sanction them for their immature antics and behavior.

Beidler v. North Thurston County School District[29] reiterates this position. In *Beidler*, the court found that the First Amendment rights of a student were violated when the school punished him for creating an off-campus website that ridiculed a school administrator.[30]

The website included images of an assistant principal having sex with Homer Simpson. The court based its decision under *Tinker* and found no evidence that the images displayed a material and substantial disruption of the work or discipline of the school. Again, although the website was offensive, no one should seriously consider its effects disruptive to a school's functioning.

These cases illustrate that school officials must beware of exercising authority too liberally under the auspices that an Internet threat is everywhere. Although the Internet makes it possible to share expressions on campus, all Internet attacks against school authority figures do not always threaten the integrity of school officials. **Freedom of expression is a powerful constitutional right.** Deference to school authority does not automatically extend beyond the schoolhouse gate, unless the harmful effect of the speech or conduct falls within school walls. *Layshock v. Hermitage School District*[31] illustrates this point. Working off campus, Layshock created a parody profile of his principal on a social networking website, mocking the principal's weight and sobriety. Although the student accessed the website from school and showed it to other students, his punishment was deemed improper. There was an insufficient nexus between the expression and the school.

Most courts apply the *Tinker* standard in any student expression case, regardless of its on- or off-campus status. As long as the expression causes a substantial disruption at the school, the expression may be censored. What appears to be important is the expression's effect on the school environment, whether it is aimed at school officials' professional roles, and whether the student as creator of the expression personally disseminated the expression on campus or intended it to make its way on campus to disrupt or disturb school students or officials.

Highlights to Remember

- Territoriality is not the sole deciding factor in determining the limitations of a school administrator's authority over student expression.
- A general rule of thumb is as follows: If a sufficient geographical nexus to the school exists, it is more likely that school officials may sanction inappropriate activity.
- School officials' authority is greater over on-campus expressions than off-campus expressions. Generally, school officials have little to no authority over off-campus student expressions.
- If, however, student speech threatens school safety in a **Columbine-like** manner, school officials may respond.

- Expressions may be sanctioned that compromise school officials' ability to perform their duties.
- School officials may intervene in student expression that substantially interferes with the work and discipline of the school. This includes the maintenance of a civil atmosphere toward school employees and students alike. Demeaning, derogatory, threatening, and sexually suggestive expressions need not be tolerated.
- School officials may appropriately discipline students if the expression realistically impairs the administration's ability to maintain control.
- Netiquette violations, while boorish and offensive, may not be sanctioned. Expressions that do not substantially disrupt the school and expressions that cannot be taken seriously should not be sanctioned.
- Freedom of expression is a powerful constitutional right. A school's authority to censor does not automatically extend beyond the schoolhouse gates, unless the harmful effect substantially falls within its walls.

Notes

1. Morse v. Frederick, 551 U.S. 393, 407 (2007).
2. J.S. et al. v. Blue Mountain School District, 593 F.3d 286, 301 (3d Cir. 2010).
3. J.S. ex rel. H.S. v. Bethlehem Area School District, 569 Pa. 638 (2002).
4. Porter v. Ascension Parish School Board, 393 F.3d 608 (5th Cir. 2004).
5. *Id.* at 611–612.
6. O.Z. v. Board of Trustees of Long Beach Unified School District, 2008 LEXIS 110409, 11 (C.D. Cal., 2008).
7. Wisniewski v. Board of Education, 494 F.3d 34, 35 (2d Cir. 2007), *cert. denied* 128 S. Ct. 1741 (2008).
8. J.S., 569 Pa. 638 (2002).
9. LaVine v. Blaine School District, 257 F.3d 981 (9th Cir. 2001), *cert. denied* 536 U.S. 959 (2002).
10. Doninger v. Niehoff, 514 F. Supp. 2d 199 (D. Conn. 2007), *affirmed* 527 F.3d 41, 52 (2d Cir. 2008).
11. Boucher v. School Board of the School District of Greenfield, 134 F.3d 821 (7th Cir. 1998).
12. Doninger, 514 F. Supp. 2d 199.
13. J.C. v. Beverly Hills Unified School District, 2010 LEXIS 54481, 27 (C.D. Cal. 2010).
14. J.S. ex rel. H.S. v. Bethlehem Area School District, 569 Pa. 638 (2002).
15. *Id.* at 865.
16. J.S. et al. v. Blue Mountain School District, 593 F.3d 286, 301 (3d Cir. 2010).
17. J.S. v. Blue Mountain School District, 2008 LEXIS 72685,18, n.4 (2008), *affirmed* 2010 U.S. LEXIS 2388 (3d Cir. 2010).
18. Requa v. Kent School District No. 415, 492 F. Supp. 2d 1272, 1273–1274 (W.D. Wa. 2007).

19. *Id.* at 1274.
20. *Id.*
21. *Id.* at 1279.
22. *Id.*
23. *Id.* at 1280.
24. Killion v. Franklin Regional School District, 136 F. Supp. 2d 446, 448 (W.D. Pa. 2001).
25. *Id.* at 455.
26. *Id.* at 456.
27. *Id.* at 456, citing Klein v. Smith, 635 F. Supp. 1440, 1442 (D. Me. 1986).
28. Papandrea, M.-R. (2008). Student speech rights in the digital age. *Florida Law Review, 60,* 1027, 1066, citing M.K. v. Three Rivers Local School District, No. 1:07CV1011, slip opinion at 5,6 (S.D. Ohio Dec. 28, 2007).
29. District pays $62,000 in damages after losing suit filed by student suspended for website. (2001). *Student Press Law Center Report, 22*(2), 24. Retrieved from http://www.splc.org/report_detail.asp?id=673&edition=18.
30. *Id.*
31. Layshock v. Hermitage School District, 496 F. Supp. 2d 587 (W.D. Pa. 2007).

8

A School's Duty to Protect

When offensive Internet content is directed toward another student, classmates, or the school's operation, the potential for a material disruption is great. Recently, courts have taken an affirmative stance against this type of behavior. Several lower courts are now holding that school officials have not only an affirmative **duty to restore and maintain order** but also a duty to **prevent the disruption** from happening at all.[1]

Generally, schools have **no duty to protect students from harm** caused by third parties, including other students. This is true even if the school is aware of reports of abuse, as was the case in the Columbine massacre situation.[2] There is no special relationship between a student and school administrators creating an affirmative duty to protect. School attendance, although compulsory, does not create a "custodial special relationship" like the one that exists in state correctional or mental health institutions, which requires or mandates protection from harm.[3]

Proximate Cause

Typically claims against schools in peer harassment cases fail under the **proximate cause** test. The student perpetrator is the proximate cause of the harm. The school is NOT! This is true even if the school is negligent in its response in handling a situation.[4] As noted in the Columbine decision, the severity of the injury does not negate the rule. In *Lawson v. City of Chicago*,[5] an Illinois court dismissed a claim against a school filed by a mother when her son was fatally shot by another student in the school. The court held that the school district owed no special duty to her son. The school district's intermittent use of metal detectors to prevent weapons from entering the school building did not override the shooter's proximate culpability for the student's death. The student shooter, not the school, was the proximate cause of harm to her son. Likewise, a school would not be liable for technology-based peer-on-peer harm. This is true even in districts that have a policy against accessing social networking websites or that provide blocking technology for Internet access. A school is not liable when a student attacks another student online by navigating around the system or abusing school resources. Again, the student offender is the proximate cause of the harm, not the school.

Foreseeability

Most claims against schools for peer harassment resulting in injury also fail under the foreseeability test. If school officials could not have reasonably foreseen the precise student's attack or harmful action, the school and its officials will not be liable for their failure to prevent a student's injury. This is true even though officials may have had some knowledge of prior conduct that has led to such injuries. This is most notably exemplified by the Columbine situation, where school officials had some advance warnings of the planned event and the exact date on which the attack was to occur. The threats were not taken seriously, and no precautions to avert the tragedy were employed. Notwithstanding those facts and the tragic resulting circumstances, no affirmative duty to protect the victims from the attack was imposed on school officials.[6]

Although rare, successful claims of foreseeability against schools do occur when the harm was foreseeable (unless state tort immunity applies) and the school demonstrated a **deliberate indifference** toward preventing it. *Mirand v. City of New York*[7] is an example of such a situation. In *Mirand*, a student who was stabbed was awarded $800,000 from the school district. The student victim reported the threat to her teacher and actively searched for a security guard, but she received no assistance. The teacher, although expressly aware of the dangerous situation, did nothing to help the victim. The school itself provided no security personnel from whom the victim could seek assistance.

The actual knowledge of the threat by the teacher and the total lack of concern provided both sufficient foreseeability and deliberate indifference to support liability.

Immunity

Finally, even if educators do have a duty to protect students from the harm of others, claims against a school for student injuries may still be dismissed based on state immunity issues. The school as a political unit of a state may be immune to tort liability based on the Eleventh Amendment to the U.S. Constitution, which "precludes the adjudication of pendent state law claims against non-consenting state defendants."[8]

Peer-on-Peer Cases

Cases in which schools have failed to protect one student from harm by another have been litigated in federal courts under the Due Process Clause. These claims, like their state counterparts, typically do not succeed. There is no substantive or procedural duty to protect individuals from harm caused by third persons who are not state actors. The only peer-on-peer harassment case that has been addressed by the Supreme Court is *Davis ex rel. LaShonda D. v. Monroe County Board of Education*,[9] and that case dealt specifically with sexual harassment under Title IX of the Education Amendments of 1972, not substantive due process. Issues regarding protection by school authorities against peer-on-peer emotional harm, physical harm, or disability-based harassment under state or federal disability laws have not been addressed by the Court.

In *Davis ex rel. LaShonda D.*, the Court held that Title IX (not due process) allows a child plaintiff to recover damages from a federally funded educational institution in a peer-on-peer sexual harassment situation when the sexual harassment of the student victim is either (1) so severe, pervasive, and objectively offensive that it undermines and detracts from the victim's educational experience, or (2) so severe and pervasive that the victim-student is effectively denied equal access to an institution's resources and opportunities. Even then, the damages against the school are limited to cases in which the school **"acts with *deliberate indifference* to known acts of harassment," and those acts have "a *systemic effect* on educational programs and activities** [emphasis added]."[10] The misconduct must occur during school hours and on school grounds or otherwise under the supervision of school employees.

The Court stressed that "damages are not available for simple acts of teasing and name-calling among school children, even where these comments target differences in gender."[11] Isolated incidents are insufficient as well. But schools do have an obligation to reasonably respond to harassment. Damages may be awarded when the school acts with deliberate indifference to the sexual misconduct of students **under their watch,** such that the student is denied equal access to education under Title IX.

LaShonda, a fifth-grade student, was awarded damages from the school under Title IX after being subjected to a classmate's sexual harassment. In this case, LaShonda demonstrated that the school was deliberately indifferent to the perpetrator's "persistent sexual advances" creating an "intimidating, hostile, offensive, and abusive school environment."[12] Here, the student, over a five-month period, repeatedly reported abusive peer-on-peer incidents to the school authorities. The school took no disciplinary action against the offender. This was in spite of the fact that the conduct continued for many months, and some incidents occurred while under the supervision of a classroom teacher. Eventually, the harassment ended when the child perpetrator pleaded guilty to sexual battery. In the meantime, LaShonda's grades dropped, and she penned a suicide note.

Although the *Davis ex rel. LaShonda D.* case does not per se extend liability to schools for other peer-on-peer harassment situations, it does provide useful guidance for use in other potential civil liability situations. Essentially, the case implies that when a school district is aware of a situation that effectively denies a student access to educational opportunities and experiences, the school district should make efforts to resolve the problem.

School districts should not just stand back and ignore the problem or repeat ineffective remedies. The case of *Annamaria M. ex rel. Antoinette M. v. Napa Valley Unified School District*[13] discusses this matter. In *Annamaria M.,* a parent, on behalf of her sexually assaulted daughter, sought damages against a school district, claiming that its habitual use of ineffective efforts amounted to deliberate indifference. The school was notified by both the child and the mother about the child's sexual harassment by two classmates. The school, however, did nothing but tell her to ignore it. The inappropriate touching and comments continued over a period of six to seven weeks. Verbal and written complaints were repeatedly filed with the school, but still the school did nothing. The child initially quit school, but eventually returned and was placed into a different class. The mother sought relief from the courts. Ultimately, the court found the school's remedial measures were deliberately indifferent, but the claim was dismissed under a sovereign immunity claim.

Recent Viable Causes of Action

The recent trend has been for courts to move away from or to ignore sovereign immunity and thus to hold schools accountable. Several recent lawsuits alleging peer-on-peer bullying harassment support viable causes of action. Gender-related harassment lawsuits under Title IX have caused schools to be financially liable. Likewise, disability lawsuits may also provide relief to victims. In *Shore Regional High School Board of Education v. P.S. ex rel. P.S.*,[14] a student with learning disabilities in the special education program was victimized for several years through name calling and physical abuse, including having bullies pull out chunks of his hair and break bones in his back and knee. Prior to his Supreme Court appointment, Justice Alito ordered the school district to reimburse P. S.'s parents for all costs incurred as a result of the lawsuit. In his ruling, Justice Alito acknowledged that "bullying does not go away on its own,"[15] thereby implying that schools have an affirmative duty to take some action to protect students against it.

A Kansas case awarded **$250,000 plus attorney fees and expenses in the amount of $268,793.51** to a child victimized from seventh through eleventh grade.[16] The child was called names, and rumors were spread about his sexual preference, which caused him to leave the school. Since it had actual knowledge of the bullying behavior and its remedial efforts were ineffective, the school was found liable. Using the same methods over and over again with no relief to the victim may cause school liability.

A 2005 New Jersey case resulted in similar liability against a school. In *L.W. v. Toms River Regional Schools*,[17] L. W. was physically abused and called "faggot," "homo," and "butt boy" by other students on a daily basis over a period of four years. The school disciplined the individual abusers, but did not make a concerted, systemic effort to stop the bullying. As a result, the school paid a **$50,000** award to L. W.

Schools cannot overlook chronic bullying, because the results may be tragic. Two additional examples occurred in Washington and Michigan. In a 1998 Washington state case, a 13-year-old boy committed suicide after he was repeatedly bullied and assaulted in school.[18] The case was settled for **$140,000**, since the school did not effectively handle the situation.

In March 2010, a Michigan court ordered a school district to pay **$800,000** to a student. The school district failed to stop a pattern of abuse against the child for several years. It is not enough that the school district sanctioned the individual student perpetrators for their bullying activities. There must also be a **concerted effort to stop systemic bullying**. This case demonstrates that schools can be held responsible for peer-on-peer harassment if enough is not done to provide a safe environment.

Although these cases do not involve cyber bullying, the result would be the same for cyber bullying cases. Schools could be liable for failure to protect students when the bullying behavior is systemic and the school's response is ineffective.

In contrast to the above cases, in *Yap v. Oceanside Union Free School District*,[19] the New York court found in favor of the school district, because it "'doggedly but unsuccessfully' attempted to address the Yaps' allegations of bullying and harassment."[20] The case involved fifth grader Yap, who was the victim of repeated racial attacks over a period of time. The principal documented each bullying incident, investigated it, and admonished the bullies. She also invoked schoolwide tolerance education, denied recess and lunch privileges, and created an antibullying curriculum, all to no avail; the bullying continued. However, because the principal had instituted **a variety of measures** to deter the bullying, she avoided liability.

Highlights to Remember

- The general rule is that schools have no duty to protect students from harm caused by third parties, including other students. No special relationship exists between a student and school officials creating an affirmative duty to protect.
- The third-party bully, not the school, is the proximate cause of the harm to a student. Third parties are therefore responsible for their actions.
- If school officials are unable to reasonably foresee the precise harm to a student, the school district will not be liable for its failure to prevent the student's injury.
- Successful claims against school districts for peer-on-peer harm are rare, but do occur when the harm is foreseeable and school officials have demonstrated a deliberate indifference toward preventing it.
- Notwithstanding state immunity issues, school districts may be liable when school officials respond with deliberate indifference to known acts of on-campus harassment. The bullying activities must (1) systemically and negatively affect the student-victim's equal access to the institution's resources and opportunities or (2) undermine or detract from the student-victim's educational experiences.
- Schools are not liable for simple acts of teasing or name-calling or for isolated bullying incidents.

- Recently, lawsuits against school districts have been upheld when systemic bullying has occurred (typically related to core characteristics, e.g., race, religion, sexual orientation, ethnicity, disability, and gender), and remedial efforts were ineffective.
- A school district's failure to stop a pattern of abuse against a child for several years often results in hefty financial settlements ($50,000 to $800,000). Schools must make a concerted effort to stop systemic bullying.

Notes

1. Lowery v. Euverard, 497 F.3d 584, 596 (6th Cir. 2007), *cert. denied* 2008 U.S. LEXIS 6449 (2008).
2. Ireland v. Jefferson County Sheriff's Dept., 193 F. Supp. 2d 1201 (D. Colo. 2002).
3. DeShaney v. Winnebago County Dept. of Social Services, 489 U.S. 189 (1989). See also Dorothy J. ex rel. Brian B. v. Little Rock School District, 7 F.3d 729, 732 (7th Cir. 1993); and Lawson v. City of Chicago, 662 N.E. 2d 1377, 1382 (Ill. App. Ct. 1996).
4. Lawes v. Board of Education of City of N.Y., 213 N.E. 2d 667 (N.Y. 1965).
5. Lawson v. City of Chicago, 662 N.E. 2d 1377 (Ill. App. Ct. 1996).
6. Ireland, 193 F. Supp. 2d at 1201.
7. Mirand v. City of New York, 637 N.E. 2d 263 (N.Y. 1994).
8. Pennhurst State School & Hospital. v. Halderman, 465 U.S. 89, 106 (1984); Raygor v. Regents of University of Minn., 534 U.S. 533, 540 (2002).
9. Davis ex rel. LaShonda D. v. Monroe County Board of Education, 526 U.S. 629 (1999).
10. *Id.* at 633.
11. *Id.* at 652.
12. *Id.* at 629.
13. Annamaria M. ex rel. Antoinette M. v. Napa Valley Unified School District, 2006 WL 1525733, 1 (N.D. Cal. 2006).
14. Shore Regional High School Board of Education v. P.S. ex rel. P.S., 381 F.3d 194 (3d Cir. 2004).
15. Conn, K. (2006, November 11). *Bullying in K–12 public schools: Searching for solutions.* Commonwealth Educational Policy Institute. Retrieved from http://www.cepionline.org/backupsite-11-01-06/policy_issues/bullying/bullying_in_k-12.html.
16. Theno v. Tonganoxie Unified School District No. 464, 377 F. Supp. 2d, 952 (D. Kan. 2005).
17. L.W. v. Toms River Regional Schools, 2005 WL 3299837 (N.J. Sup. A.D. 2005).
18. Dawson, D. (2006, July 31). Girls take school to court, saying it ignored bullying. ABC News. Retrieved from http://abcnews.go.com/print?id=2256089.
19. Yap v. Oceanside Union Free School District, 303 F. Supp. 2d 284 (E.D. N.Y. 2004).
20. *Id.* at 296.

9

Proactive Approaches to Cyber Bullying

In addition to the case law precedent for reactive handling of cyber bullying incidents, many states and schools are employing proactive measures to prevent cyber bullying. To that end, many new laws, procedures, and practices have been created and enacted to discourage bullying types of behavior. Some include technological limitations and disablement measures, some include student-parent-school contracts based upon acceptable use policies (AUPs), and some include criminal or criminal-like sanctions for engaging in cyber bullying behavior. Inappropriate expressions may subject students not only to school discipline but also to criminal punishment or civil liability.

Not all forms of cyber bullying are actionable, as case law indicates. Distinguishing free expression from censorable online behavior poses its own issues. The lack of uniformity between individual state definitions and federal definitions exacerbates the problem. Certain categories of harassments, true threats, aggressive expressions, and stalking behaviors may provide **causes of action**; whereas parodies, political commentaries, obnoxious activities, or rude and uncivil behavior may not. For example, peer-on-peer harassment envelops many forms, ranging from subtle teasing, name calling, referencing physical characteristics, and racial epithets to referencing sexual preferences. Under federal law, **harassment establishes a cause of action**

only when based on race, ethnicity, gender, religion, or disability, and then only when those harassing acts have a systemic effect on educational programs and activities.[1]

Legislative Approaches

Other definitional disparities result from state statutes. For example, the California Education Code is distinctive in that it extends students' free speech rights while on campus to the same extent those rights may be exercised outside of the school context.[2] Consequently, different outcomes may result when evaluating violations of students' free speech rights under federal and state laws. Some states, like Illinois, have created a **cause of action** (cyber stalking) when, through a repeated course of conduct (on at least two separate occasions), a person harasses, alarms, torments, or terrorizes another person with a threat of immediate or future harm through the use of electronic communication.[3] Other states, like New York, provide a **cause of action** without the requirement for repetition. New York's Penal Law Section 240.30 defines aggravated harassment in the second degree as follows:

> A person is guilty of aggravated harassment in the second degree when, with intent to harass, annoy, threaten or alarm another person, he or she: 1. Either (a) communicates with a person, anonymously or otherwise by telephone, or by telegraph, mail, or any other form of written communication, in a manner likely to cause annoyance or alarm; or (b) causes a communication to be initiated by mechanical or electronic means or otherwise, with a person, anonymously or otherwise, by telephone, or by telegraph, mail or any other form of written communication, in a manner likely to cause annoyance or alarm; or 2. Makes a telephone call, whether or not a conversation ensues, with no purpose of legitimate communication. . . .[4]

Notwithstanding state and federal variations, most experts have attempted to define and regulate cyber bullying along the same lines as traditional bullying. The only difference is the medium of expression. Thus, they attempt to resolve cyber aggression situations by using the same methodologies imposed for traditional bullying— **fitting the square peg in the round hole.**

Community Practices

One of the most noteworthy challenges in dealing with bullying and cyber bullying cases is the reality that from jurisdiction to jurisdiction and from school to school, enforcement and disciplinary practices vary. Some localities practice strict enforcement, while others ignore or respond with leniency. A recent case from Pennsylvania concerning the practice of sexting demonstrates this point. In *Miller et al. v. Skumanick*,[5] the court dealt with the topic of sexting, a practice of sending or posting sexually explicit text messages and images via a cellular telephone or over the Internet. The school discovered that male students had been trading pictures of scantily clad and nude teenage girls over their cell phones. The school then confiscated the phones and turned them over to the prosecutor.

The prosecutor notified the youngsters who owned the cell phones that they all could be prosecuted for possessing or distributing child pornography, in violation of the Pennsylvania statute. He further advised them that the crimes were felonies and could subject the offenders to registration as sex offenders or to having their names and pictures posted on the state's sex offender website. The prosecutor threatened the alleged offenders—both the boys who had traded the pictures and the girls who had posed for them—and their parents with prosecution unless the children submitted to an informal adjustment regime that would include probation, successfully completing a six- to nine-month program focused on education and counseling, and payment of a $100 program fee.

A female student's parent objected and questioned whether or not his daughter's picture was provocative. The picture was taken when she was 13; it showed her and her friend wearing white opaque bras while speaking on a phone. The prosecutor's response was that the girls were accomplices in the production of child pornography in that they allowed themselves to be photographed. The girls' parents filed suit, seeking an order enjoining the prosecutor from initiating criminal charges against them, since the images did not depict sexual activity or exhibit the genitals in a lascivious way. The girls asserted, among other things, that even if one assumes the photos were provocative, provocative photos do not qualify as depictions of prohibited sexual acts under the Pennsylvania statute. Hence the photos were not illegal, even though they involved minors. The court agreed with the girls and granted the temporary restraining order prohibiting the filing of criminal charges.

In this case, the school and the prosecutor took the matter seriously and vigorously pursued remedies. Not all jurisdictions respond quite so aggressively. As previously discussed, many jurisdictions are seeking alternative remedies or a calibrated response to the offensive behavior.

School Codes and Acceptable Use Policies

Traditionally, criminalization and limitation of expression violates the First Amendment regardless of whether it is done in person, in writing, or over the Internet, except in a few limited areas.[6] Overly broad statutes and policies are forbidden, as are most policies and practices controlling content over form or content over restrictions on time, place, and manner of communication. Nevertheless, many attempts to regulate expression, including cyber or electronic expression, have been initiated.

Under First Amendment jurisprudence, limitation of expression is acceptable if it is **content neutral**. Speech may be restricted as to the time, place, and manner of delivery, as long as the government's purpose in regulating serves purposes unrelated to the content of expression. If the speech has an incidental effect on some speakers or messages but not on others, it may still be regulated. Recognized as special environments, schools may limit the time, place, and manner of inappropriate expression.

It is entirely permissible for school leaders to ban all cell phones or to restrict access to personal websites during the school day. These actions would not violate First Amendment principles, because content-neutral regulations on time, place, and manner are tolerable.[7] Some schools have imposed total bans on technology, others restrict access to social networks, and still others limit the purposes for and places where students may use technology. Limitations come with the following drawbacks:

1. They limit access to valuable academic resources.
2. They prevent certain educational opportunities.
3. Some objectionable information still filters through.

Schools that have attempted to limit access to technology have found that students still find a way to beat the system. Students are able to surreptitiously access websites on personal devices. Forbidden content and information are often discussed or brought onto campus through means other than the school's computers. For an example, refer to the case of *Requa v. Kent School District No. 415.*[8] The Kent School District was diligent in its efforts to control student access to inappropriate materials. District computers were specifically configured to prevent student access to social websites. Yet in this case, a student posted a "booty" video during the summer concerning a teacher. Months later, the video made its way to school via the news media. The court found that the video had substantially impacted the school environment.

It is impossible to prevent information from coming on campus or to control its arrival. Rather than imposing an absolute ban on all technology use within an educational setting, most schools have established codes and policies that discourage, prohibit, or prevent bullying conduct. With the introduction of technology as a format for electronic harassment by students, many schools have simply amended their policies to include the term *cyber* within this framework. Some schools and regional education offices have chosen to institute practices designed to block access and closely monitor Internet and cyber activities.

Additionally, a considerable number of schools have adopted acceptable use policies (AUPs) for school computer usage, making it a contractual issue between the school and the student.[9] One such example involves a school district in Libertyville, Illinois, that requires students to sign a pledge agreeing that **illegal and inappropriate Internet usage or postings** could disqualify them from participation in extracurricular activities.[10] The legality of these policies, or more specifically, the legality of the enforcement of these school policies, creates much debate and spawns extensive and expensive litigation. Establishing acceptable limitations on free speech concerning cyber usage among students requires precise wording and equitable implementation of all policies and rules. **Enforcement will be permissible only as long as it is narrowly confined, reasonable, and designed to further the mission of the school.**

Disputes and litigation have resulted as to what amounts to inappropriate Internet usage or postings. Vaguely worded or **overly broad** antiharassment policies that prohibit a wide range of speech offensive to others have been held to violate the First Amendment. Policies are overly broad if there is a substantial likelihood that the policy itself will inhibit free expression.[11] The Third Circuit Court of Appeals unanimously supported an **overbreadth** claim by two high school students, who claimed that the school district's antiharassment policy violated their First Amendment rights.[12] Specifically, the Pennsylvania policy prohibited harassment and provided examples, including "any unwelcome verbal, written or physical conduct which offends, denigrates, or belittles an individual" because of "race, religion, color, national origin, gender, sexual orientation, disability, or other personal characteristics."[13] Citing this policy, school officials sanctioned students who voiced their religious belief that homosexuality was a sin. Judge Samuel A. Alito Jr.[14] writing the opinion for the court, slammed the school for its action and claimed, "No court or legislature has ever suggested that unwelcome speech directed at another's 'values' may be prohibited under the rubric of anti-discrimination."[15]

Using the *Saxe* case as precedent, school codes that crudely or broadly define cyber bullying to include any unwelcome slurs based on one's actual or perceived race, religion, color, national origin, gender, sexual orientation, disability, or other personal characteristics will most likely not be upheld. Cyber bullying activities that offend, denigrate, or belittle a child by "derogatory remarks, jokes, demeaning comments or behaviors, slurs, mimicking, name calling, graffiti, innuendo, gestures, physical contact, stalking, threatening, bullying, extorting or the display or circulation of written material or pictures"[16] may also result in successful challenges if regulated or censored. While all of these activities are offensive and may create a health risk or interfere with a student's educational performance, not all constitute actionable conduct (cause of action) by school authorities under state or federal law. **There is no categorical "harassment exception," "bullying exception," or "mean spirited exception" to the First Amendment's free speech clause.**[17]

Overly broad or imprecise and vague policies that prohibit a substantial amount of speech that would not constitute actionable harassment under either federal or state law will not be upheld as an enforceable school policy. Although the codes that prohibit such conduct may not necessarily withstand constitutional attack, specific speech or expressions that substantially disrupt school operations or interfere with the right of others may still be regulated.

The recent case of *Flaherty v. Keystone Oaks School District*[18] supports this premise. Therein, a student, in accordance with the policies set forth in the school student handbook, was prohibited from using school computers and participating in afterschool activities, including the volleyball team. Using his home computer, he posted a critical online message mocking one of his teachers and a teammate.

The student claimed that the school policy concerning the use of school computers was unconstitutionally vague and overbroad. Upon review, the court agreed with the student and found that the school had overstepped its boundaries of censorship. In other words, the school district violated the student's First Amendment rights when it sought to discipline him because of the messages he posted on a website message board. Citing the *Saxe* decision, the court found that the language of the message fell outside the scope of lewd, vulgar, or profane language (*Fraser*) or school-sponsored speech (*Hazelwood*). Thus, the message had to pass the substantial disruption test (*Tinker*) to justify censorship. Since the school failed to meet that challenge, the student's rights had been violated. Ultimately the school settled the case for **$100,000.**[19]

Another case supporting this rule that schools cannot have overly broad policies to limit school expression is *Nuxoll v. Indian Prairie School District #204.*[20] A Naperville, Illinois, student brought suit against his high school, claiming that the school's policy banning derogatory comments (referring to race, ethnicity, religion, sexual orientation, or disability) was unconstitutional. Specifically, the student protested the school's policy forbidding him to make negative comments about homosexuality. He was not allowed to wear a shirt bearing the words *Be Happy, Not Gay*. The school claimed the comment was derogatory toward a particular sexual orientation and thus was inappropriate in a school setting. Judge Posner thoroughly rejected that argument, stating that schools cannot "prohibit derogatory comments in order to protect the rights of the students against whom [they] are directed."[21] Schools do not have a legal right to prevent criticism of beliefs or a way of life.[22] Furthermore, nothing about the statement was defamatory or indicated that it was directed toward a specific individual. These cases make clear that **AUPs have to be narrowly confined, reasonable, and designed to further the mission of the school**.

To combat the unconstitutionally vague and overbroad language requirement, the National Education Association (NEA) suggests that an effective AUP should contain the following six key elements:

1. a preamble,
2. a definition section,
3. a policy statement,
4. an acceptable uses section,

5. an unacceptable uses section, and
6. a violations/sanctions section.

The NEA recommends that all terms be precisely defined, so that students and parents fully understand what conduct, postings, network sites, technology applications, activities, and so forth are permissible and which are off limits or beyond educational purposes. The AUP should also discuss how violations are reported and handled and to whom questions should be addressed. The signed AUP becomes a contract between the student, the parent, and the school.[23] AUPs must be flexible enough to accommodate the changes in technology and specific enough to prevent threats to students.

Students must understand the value of technology as a tool, but also, students must be cognizant of its risks. At a minimum, **all AUPs should be reviewed regularly** to ensure they meet current state and federal guidelines and address new technological concerns. The No Child Left Behind Act, the Children's Internet Protection Act, and the Enhancing Education Through Technology provision of the Elementary and Secondary Education Act require that all schools receiving federal assistance for technology have a safety policy and a technology protection measure in place. These requirements protect children from accessing or being exposed to harmful depictions, including materials that are obscene or contain child pornography or any materials harmful to minors.

One example of an AUP that passed constitutional muster was discussed in the Tenth Circuit case of *West v. Derby Unified School District No. 260*.[24] The adopted policy reads, in part, as follows:

> District employees and student(s) shall not racially harass or intimidate another student(s) by name calling, using racial or derogatory slurs, wearing or possession of items depicting or implying racial hatred or prejudice. District employees and *students shall not at school, on school property or at school activities wear or have in their possession any written material, either printed or in their own handwriting, that is racially divisive or creates ill will or hatred.* (Examples: clothing, articles, material, publications or *any item that denotes* Ku Klux Klan, Aryan Nation–White Supremacy, Black Power, *Confederate flags* or articles, Neo-Nazi or any other "hate" group. This list is not intended to be all inclusive.)[25]

The *West* case allowed restrictions of depictions of Confederate flags because of its recognized relationship to prior acts of on-campus violence, not specifically as a prior restraint on content.

Other Legislative Enactments

On a wider or more global level, legislatures have also introduced bills and instituted programs designed to reduce aggressive cyber conduct. Over half of the states and the federal government have passed or are considering passing anti–cyber bullying legislation. Unlike the school policies discussed previously, this legislation does not attempt to specify or define what conduct is illegal but instead directs the school districts to amend their existing antibullying procedures to include cyber activities. Furthermore, none of these enactments or proposals creates a new right or cause of action. The legislation merely encourages schools to create policies to curb the offensive behavior.

Courts recognize that the free speech clause is not absolute and that limitations exist; hence, legislation may, to a limited extent, restrict certain forms of free speech.[26] Historically, certain conduct by statute or by case law has been upheld as unprotected by the First Amendment. Obscenity,[27] defamation,[28] "clear and present danger,"[29] "fighting words,"[30] and "threats" are traditionally unprotected categories of expression.[31] Society permits these few restrictions upon the content of speech, because they are "of such slight social value as a step to truth that any benefit that may be derived from them is clearly outweighed by the social interest in order and morality."[32]

In light of the permissible limitation governing speech, and cognizant of the pervasiveness and potential harm resulting from cyber aggression, 45 states have passed antibullying laws.[33] Not all provide equal guidance or deal with cyber or peer-on-peer situations. State legislation runs the gamut.[34] Some acts require mandatory reporting and notification of incidents, some provide for disciplinary sanctions for off- and on-campus incidents, and some include provisions establishing bullying prevention programs. Some include cyber bullying in legislation dealing with gang prevention, some apply it to Internet bullying if a school computer is involved,[35] and others include it under the umbrella of bullying behavior. Most of the legislation directs school districts to amend their current definition of bullying to include cyber activities and encourages the creation of antibullying policies to study or to curb the behavior.

A review of selected state legislation provides guidance in the development of district policy. The review provides suggestions for the ten best practices that districts would be advised to consider when creating or updating their district policy:

1. Require school districts to establish a policy on bullying prevention.[36]
2. Create a mechanism for confidentially reporting incidents of bullying.[37]
3. Include students and parents in the creation of the policy.[38]
4. Investigate and report all observed incidents of bullying.[39]
5. Distribute the school's antibullying policy to all students, parents, faculty, and staff.[40]
6. Report all confirmed instances of bullying to the state department of education.[41]
7. Require school districts to develop an Internet safety curriculum. The curriculum should accomplish two purposes: (1) to educate students about the dangers of posting personal information on a website and (2) to develop a plan for the prevention and reporting of bullying behavior over the Internet.[42]
8. Provide a minimum of two hours of Internet safety instruction each year for all students.[43] Their Internet safety instruction should include (1) recognizing and reporting cyber bullying behavior and (2) safe and responsible use of social networking websites, chat rooms, and other methods of Internet communication.[44]
9. Prohibit bullying behavior that disrupts the school's educational environment or occurs at school-sanctioned events, either on or off campus.[45]
10. Define protected classes such as homosexual students, religious sects, and racial minorities.[46]

Legislation will, however, bring more awareness to the problem and offer procedures, programs, and policies to follow, to educate, to document, and to handle cyber situations. Most enacted and proposed legislation is designed to accomplish that end. The mandates assist public schools in developing policy concerning education, parental involvement, intervention, procedures for disseminating bullying reporting protocol, and procedures for investigating bullying behavior at schools and elsewhere.

Federal Legislation

Federal legislation impacts a school's ability to respond to cyber bullying incidents. Federal hate crime legislation prohibits the willful injury to, intimidation of, interference with, or attempted intimidation of an individual by force or threat of force, "because of his race, color, religion or national origin."[47] Students complaining of harassment based on disability may allege violations of

- the Individuals with Disabilities Education Act (IDEA),[48]
- the Rehabilitation Act (RA),[49] or
- the Americans with Disabilities Act of 1990 (ADA).[50]

Victims of cyber bullying may have a federal cause of action based on race, ethnicity, gender, religion, or disability. On the other hand, claims of harassment based on a personal characteristic such as physical stature may be difficult to sustain. A Connecticut case provides an example.[51] The parents of Jeremy Smith, a 4'7" 75-pound high school freshman, attempted to sue school officials after their son was harassed due to his diminutive stature. Peers repeatedly bullied Jeremy by teasing and physical assaults, including stuffing him into a backpack and parading him through the school corridors. The parents claimed that the school was aware of the daily harassment, failed to protect their son, and thus violated his rights under 42 U.S.C., section 1983. However, the court found that the right to education was not a fundamental constitutional right, and section 1983 offered no protection.

Schools have their hands tied, although parents turn to the school to stop offensive expression with the hope that school discipline will eradicate the bullying behavior. Since the Supreme Court decision in *Tinker* and its progeny, the First Amendment prevents public school officials from censoring most student speech. Federal legislation is of little assistance. Current legislation supports free speech. In other words, **schools are damned if they do and damned if they don't!**

In this era of cyber technology, the pedagogical concern of school safety cannot be allowed to automatically override a student's First Amendment right to free speech regardless of where the expression originated. Off-campus origination of the threat will not automatically exempt the threat from control or censorship by the school. Schools must carefully examine the comments of students made in person or over the Internet, on school property, or by the use of school equipment, and then sanction only those who clearly exceed constitutional limits. Schools face a challenging task.

Highlights to Remember

- Not all forms of cyber bullying are sanctionable. State and federal differences in definitions complicate the issue. Consequently, evaluation of student free speech rights under federal and varying state laws may reveal different requirements depending upon jurisdiction.
- Not all state laws provide equal guidance to schools in dealing with cyber bullying or peer-on-peer situations. Some states require and have created mechanisms for reporting incidents. Some states mandate investigations. Most states require school districts to develop Internet safety curricula. Others mandate that the schools' antibullying policies be distributed to students, parents, faculty, and staff. These differences in state and federal legislation require each school district to assume responsibility for determining appropriateness under their jurisdiction.
- Community practices further complicate or challenge a school's authority to censor student expression. Local customs may dictate which cyber bullying behavior(s) are tolerated and which are not.
- Expressions may be restricted as to time, place, and manner, as long as the school's purpose in regulating is content neutral. However, these restrictions may limit access to valuable or important educational resources or opportunities, and objectionable information may filter through anyway. School officials should not underestimate the abilities of students to beat the system.
- Acceptable use policies (AUPs) are enforceable when they are narrowly confined, reasonable, and designed to further the mission of the school. Vaguely worded or overly broad policy statements violate the First Amendment.
- No categorical harassment exception, bullying exception, or mean-spirited exception exists under the First Amendment.
- Students must be instructed as to the value of technology and its inherent risks.
- All AUPs should be regularly reviewed to ensure currency regarding technological developments and alignment with state and federal guidelines.
- Schools face the challenging tasks of carefully reviewing student expression and sanctioning only those expressions that clearly exceed Constitutional limitations.

Notes

1. Davis ex rel. LaShonda D. v. Monroe County Board of Education, 526 U.S. 629 (1999).
2. Cal. Educ. Code §§ 48907 and 48950 (LexisNexis 2009).

3. 720 Ill. Comp. Stat. 5/12–7.5 (2009).

4. N. Y. Penal Law Ch. 40, § 240.30 (Penal Law Web). Aggravated harassment in the second degree. Retrieved July 29, 2009, from http://wings.buffalo.edu/law/bclc/web/NewYork/ny3(b).htm.

5. Miller et al. v. Skumanick, No. 3:09cv540 (M.D. Pa. March 30, 2009).

6. R.A.V. v. St. Paul, 505 U.S. 377, 382–383 (1992).

7. Ward v. Rock Against Racism, 491 U.S. 781, 791 (1989).

8. Requa v. Kent School District No. 415, 492 F. Supp. 2d 1272 (W.D. Wa. 2007).

9. Limber, S., & Small, M. (2003). State laws and policies to address bullying in schools. *School Psychology Review, 32*, 445, 447.

10. Associated Press. (May 23, 2006). *District to watch students on MySpace.* Retrieved from http://www.msnbc.msn.com/id/12937962.

11. Saxe v. State College Area School District, 240 F.3d 200, 214 (3d Cir. 2001).

12. *Id.*

13. *Id.* at 202–203.

14. After he penned this opinion, Justice Samuel Alito Jr. was appointed to the U.S. Supreme Court in January 2006.

15. Saxe, 240 F.3d at 210.

16. *Id.* at 203.

17. *Id.*

18. Flaherty v. Keystone Oaks School District, 247 F. Supp. 2d 698 (W.D. Pa. 2003).

19. American Civil Liberties Union. (Feb. 26, 2003). *PA court says school's punishment for Internet speech violated student's rights.* Press Release. Retrieved from http://www.aclu.org/privacy/youth/15172prs20030226.html.

20. Nuxoll v. Indian Prairie School District #204, 523 F.3d 668 (7th Cir. 2008).

21. *Id.* at 672.

22. *Id.*

23. Cromwell, S. (1998). *Getting started on the Internet: Developing an acceptable use policy (AUP).* Updated October 16, 2007. Retrieved from http://www.educationworld.com/a_curr/curr093.shtml.

24. West v. Derby Unified School District No. 260, 206 F.3d 1358 (10th Cir. 2000).

25. West, 206 F.3d at 1361.

26. Virginia v. Black, 538 U.S. 343, 358–359 (2003).

27. Roth v. United States, 354 U.S. 476 (1957); Miller v. California, 413 U.S. 15 (1973).

28. Beauharnais v. Illinois, 343 U.S. 250 (1952).

29. People v. Dietze, 549 N.E. 2d 1166, 1170 (N.Y. 1989).

30. Chaplinsky v. New Hampshire, 315 U.S. 568 (1942).

31. R.A.V. v. St. Paul, 505 U.S. 377, 381 (1992).

32. Chaplinsky, 315 U.S. at 572.

33. Bully Police USA. http://www.bullypolice.org.

34. High, B. (n.d.). *Making the grade: How states "graded" on their anti bullying laws.* Bully Police USA. Retrieved from http://www.bullypolice.org/grade.html.

35. Bully Police USA. (n.d.). *Washington State A-.* Retrieved from http://www.bullypolice.org/wa_law.html.

36. School Bullying Prevention Act, H.B. 7, Del. 114th Gen. Assembly (2007). Retrieved from http://legis.delaware.gov/LIS/lis144.nsf/vwLegislation/HB+7/$file/legis.html?open. Safe School Climate Act, A353, R400, H3573, S.C. 116th Gen. Assembly (2006). Retrieved from http://www.scstatehouse.gov/sess116_2005-2006/bills/3573.htm.

37. H. B. 2368, Ariz. 47th Leg. (2005). Retrieved from http://www.bullypolice.org/az_law.html.

38. Grim, J. (2008, Spring). The best of Barry: Barry student article: Peer harassment in our schools: Should teachers and administrators join the fight? *Barry Law Review, 10,* 155.

39. *Id.*

40. School Bullying Prevention Act, *supra* note 36.

41. *Id.*

42. See, for example, News Report. (2007, December 17). *Illinois attorney general announces cyberbullying training.* Retrieved from http://www.govtech.com/gt/articles/219244?utm_source=newsletter&utm_medium=email&utm_campaign=GTSN_2007_12_17.

43. *Id.*

44. Internet Safety Education Act, S.B. 1472, Ill. 95th Gen. Assembly (2007). Retrieved from http://www.ilga.gov/legislation/billstatus.asp?DocNum=1472&GAID=9&GA=95&DocTypeID=SB&LegID=29564&SessionID=51.

45. An act relating to including cyberbullying in school district harassment prevention policies, S.B. 5288, Wa. St. Leg. (2008). Retrieved from http://apps.leg.wa.gov/billinfo/summary.aspx?year=2007&bill=5288.

Model policy and guidance for prohibiting harassment, intimidation and bullying on school property, at school-sponsored functions and on school buses, N.J.S.A. 18A:37-13 et seq. N.J. St. Leg. (2002, rev. November, 2008). Retrieved from http://www.state.nj.us/education/parents/bully.htm.

An act to define bullying; to include cyberbullying in public school district antibullying policies, H.B. 1072, Ark. 86th Gen. Assembly (2007). Retrieved from http://www.arkleg.state.ar.us/assembly/2007/R/Bills/HB1072.pdf.

46. Jeffrey Johnson Stand Up for All Students Act, H.B. 669, Fla. House Rep. (2008). Retrieved from http://myfloridahouse.gov/Sections/Bills/billsdetail.aspx?BillId=38076&SessionIndex=1&SessionId=57&BillText=jeffrey%20johnston&BillNumber=&BillSponsorIdex=0&BillListIndex=0&BillStatuteText=&BillTypeIndex=0&BillReferredIndex=0&HouseChamber=H&BillSearchIndex=0.

47. 18 U.S.C. § 245(b)(2) (2000).

48. 20 U.S.C. § 1400 (2000),

49. 29 U.S.C. § 794 (2000).

50. 42 U.S.C. § 12101 (2000).

51. Smith v. Guilford Board of Education, 2005 WL 3211449 (D. Conn. Nov. 30, 2005).

PART II

Lessons Learned and Rules to Live By

10

Four Lessons Learned From Experience

School administrators often believe they need to resolve all problems of their students and staff. However, reacting to all cyber situations is not necessarily the best approach. Often the knee-jerk response or the gut reaction may be inappropriate. Instead, administrators must determine if the cyber bullying expression falls within one of the specific categories exempt from First Amendment protection. The categories exempt from First Amendment protection in a school setting include

1. certain criminal and civil conduct;
2. acceptable use policy violations;
3. expressions that substantially and materially disrupt the educational institution;
4. expressions that interfere with the rights of others;
5. expressions that are lewd, vulgar, indecent, and plainly offensive;
6. expressions that are contrary to legitimate pedagogical concerns; and
7. expressions that reflect antisocial civic violations.

If the expression falls within one of these enumerated categories, then the administrator may respond. If the expression does not fit within one of these categories, school administrators must refrain from taking action against the student offender. If no exemption from free speech exists, administrators may **not** sanction the offender—no matter how much they want to, how personal the situation becomes, or what moral or external pressures are applied.

Lesson 1: Cyber Censoring Mistakes Are Costly

The first lesson learned from Part I is that schools cannot afford to make cyber censoring mistakes. Many of the cases discussed therein involved situations where the courts determined that the student expression did **not** fall within one of the categories exempt from First Amendment protection in a school setting. As a result, in eight of the cases, financial penalties were levied against the schools for their violation of students' First Amendment rights. Public schools cannot afford to pay out large sums of money (in these cases, $50,000 to $800,000) to individual students. The deductible and the increase in future insurance premiums impact school budgets even if the penalties are paid by district insurance companies.

One of the tenets of a quality education is the necessity to encourage an open dialogue, question and assess ideas, and challenge existing views. Schools should provide the forum and opportunity for students to demonstrate these tenets. The inappropriate and overly broad school censorship of expression interferes with this notion.

Only actual or realistic potential categorical violations should be sanctioned. True threats, based upon a past record of disturbance or the actual ability to carry them out, may be sanctioned. **ONLY lewd, vulgar, indecent, or plainly offensive expressions created and or disseminated on school campuses before inappropriate-age audiences may be sanctioned.** Further, schools may sanction nonroutine disruptions caused by cyber expressions, **not** disruptions caused or instigated by the administration's response to the expressions.

Lesson 2: Schools Have Options Beyond Censorship

The second lesson learned from Part I is that **just because all offensive student cyber expressions cannot be censored does not mean that administrators can do nothing.** What administrators can do is to take their gut reaction and channel it into positive academic and emotional learning experiences. Administrators can

- modify and manipulate their existing articulated curricula to teach appropriate social skills and responsibilities;
- promote activities that teach students how to appropriately express themselves and their viewpoints; and
- create a healthy culture and climate that supports the constitutional provisions as related to fairness, respect, and equality for all.

Lesson 3: Administrators Must Provide Justification for Their Actions

A third lesson learned from the cases discussed in Part I is that administrators must be able to justify their actions when sanctioning students for their expressions. Administrators must provide sufficient reasons to support their actions. These reasons may include the amount of time and personnel devoted to resolve situations, the historical background supporting a belief that disruptions may occur, and any connections between the expression and its effect upon school operations.

In addition to justifying the specific response, administrators must also determine if their particular response corrects the overall problem. Administrators must address not only the source of the problem but the underlying causes of the problem. Schools cannot ignore the complexities of the issue by treating it with a simple bandage when surgery is required. Administrators have a responsibility to sanction individual offenders and prevent systemic problems from reoccurring.

Lesson 4: Cyber Sanctioning Should Fairly and Equitably Fit the Offense

A fourth lesson gleaned from Part II focuses on what discipline is appropriate for a particular situation. Schools should carefully consider what sanctions to apply based on the level of the offensive expression and the student's background. Similarly situated students should be treated fairly and equally for comparable expression violations. Not every situation requires students to be expelled or suspended. Comparable expression violations with similar student experiences should result in similar sanctions. For example, where two students with comparable backgrounds use similar offensive expressions, one student should not receive a 30-day suspension and another student a two-year expulsion. Administrators should weigh the sanctions according to the severity of the incident, the student's school history, and the cause and amount of disruption.

Most of the cases discussed whether a sanction could be applied at all. However, the *Doninger v. Niehoff*[1] case dealt with the level of administrative response. In *Doninger*, a junior class secretary was upset and frustrated by the school officials' decision to reschedule a music festival that she as a member of the student council had worked hard in planning. She blogged about her concerns on her publicly accessible social networking website. Included in the blog were disparaging names such as "douchebag" for her school principal, vulgar and misleading comments, and requests for students and parents to contact the school to complain. School personnel met with the student and specifically told her that appealing directly to the public was not an appropriate method of resolving complaints.[2] Her actions caused the school to receive an influx of calls and e-mails. Students became all riled up, a sit-in was threatened, and administrators missed or were late to school-related activities.[3] School officials punished her by disqualifying her from running for class secretary during her senior year.

In reviewing the correctness of the decision to discipline, the court drew a clear line between student activity that affects matters of "legitimate concern to the school community" and student activity that does not.[4] Here the student's off-campus blog posting affected a legitimate school concern. Critical to allowing the school to discipline her was the limitation of discipline to her extracurricular activity. The student contravened one of the school's pedagogical missions when she abused her position as a student government leader. Her insubordination resulted in the court finding a reasonably foreseeable disruption to the school's work under *Tinker*.

The court seemed to imply that although schools generally do not have a right to intervene in off-campus, non–school-sponsored activities, they may issue school consequences to a student (1) if the consequence substantially impacts academic performance, or (2) if the student expression causes a substantial disruption to the school's work.

Here the student's actions as a student leader undermined the educators' role of instilling civility and cooperative conflict resolution. It is well established that the school's role is to promote good citizenship in and out of school.[5] Extracurricular activities such as student government promote this role. School administrators can issue school-related consequences for inappropriate behavior associated with the student's recognized responsibilities. Effective education depends on teachers controlling the focus of particular assignments and learning activities. "Learning is more vital in the classroom than free speech."[6] This is also evident in the *Settle v. Dickson County School Board* case, in which a teacher refused to accept a paper titled "The Life of Jesus," because the student failed to follow the instructions for the assignment.[7] Teachers retain control over matters of curriculum, course content, and school-related extracurricular activities.[8]

Doninger advised that school officials have broad latitude in determining whether students are permitted to participate in extracurricular activities.[9] Participation is a privilege rather than a right.[10] Participation may be rescinded when students fail to comply with or abuse the obligations inherent in the activities.[11] It is important that the consequences for inappropriate expression be limited to the instructional responsibilities of the school. A different, more serious consequence than disqualification from student office may have raised constitutional concerns.

The First Amendment provides that "Congress shall make no law . . . abridging the freedom of speech." However, public school students do not automatically possess unlimited First Amendment rights in school. Schools have the authority to limit student expression pursuant to "the special characteristics of the school environment."[12] The Supreme Court cases have identified those situations where schools have authority over student cyber expression.

Notes

1. Doninger v. Niehoff, 527 F.3d 41 (2d Cir. 2008), *summary judgment granted in part, summary judgment denied in part* 2009 LEXIS 2704 (D. Conn. Jan. 15, 2009).
2. *Id.* at 45.
3. *Id.* at 51.
4. *Id.* at 48.
5. *Id.* at 52.
6. *Id.* at 156.
7. Settle v. Dickson County School Board, 53 F.3d 152 (6th Cir. 1995).
8. *Id.*
9. Doninger v. Niehoff, 527 F.3d 41 (2d Cir. 2008), *summary judgment granted, in part, summary judgment denied, in part* 2009 LEXIS 2704 (D. Conn. Jan. 15, 2009).
10. *Id.* at 285.
11. *Id.* at 52.
12. Bethel School District No. 403 v. Fraser, 478 U.S. 675, 687–688 (1986).

11

Top Ten Rules That Govern School Authority Over Student Cyber Expressions

Although conflicting court decisions have surfaced and jurisdictional variations exist, the following general principles guiding cyber bullying situations have emerged from court precedent:

1. First Amendment provisions apply to public school students.
2. Censorship is permissible if the student expression reasonably suggests a substantial disruption to school activities.
3. Censorship is permissible if the student expression actually interferes with students' rights to educational benefits or substantially detracts from the learning environment.
4. Lewd, vulgar, or profane language is inappropriate in a public educational environment.[1]
5. Reasonable regulations may be imposed with respect to the time, place, and manner of student expressions involving school property, school equipment, or school events.

6. Schools may regulate school-sponsored expression if the expression is viewed as endorsed by the institution.
7. Schools may regulate school-sponsored expression on the basis of any legitimate pedagogical concern.
8. Off-campus expressions may be regulated only when a sufficient nexus to campus is shown.
9. Expression may be restricted if it is reasonably perceived to be inconsistent with the "shared values of a civilized social order."[2]
10. True threats and criminal activity may always be regulated regardless of whether they originated on or off campus.

These Top Ten Rules, like the First Amendment right from which they come, are not absolute. Exceptions exist. Further, the Rules do not exist in a vacuum. The Rules should be viewed within the context of each other and as stand-alones. In general, the Rules provide a strong framework within which school leaders may act.

Rule 1: First Amendment Provisions Apply to Public School Students

Students have First Amendment rights. They have the right to express opinions on controversial topics and maintain individual viewpoints. Students have the right to express themselves freely off campus on their own time. Parents control student expressions off campus. They have not delegated their authority to schools. However, students do not possess unlimited First Amendment rights in public schools. If more than a de minimis connection between the speech and the schools exists, schools have the power and duty to intervene. Schools have the authority to "inculcate the habits and manners of civility."[3] The age, maturity, and cognitive development of both the offender and the audience are critical factors in censoring student speech. More censorship of expression is allowed for younger and less mature students. The school's purpose involves more learning than debate at lower grade levels. *Tinker* and its progeny suggest that students retain First Amendment rights, but those rights are restricted to what is appropriate for the care and tutelage of children.[4]

Rule 2: Censorship Is Permissible if the Student Expression Reasonably Suggests a Substantial Disruption to School Activities

Student expression may be sanctioned if the school can reasonably forecast that the expression will cause a substantial disruption to school activities. The seminal court case, *Tinker*, allows students to make silent, passive, political expressions that do not cause disorder or disturbance at school.[5] It is not permissible to sanction student expression based on a desire to avoid unpleasantness or prevent the expression of unpopular viewpoints. Schools do not need to wait for a disruption to start if they can forecast a disruption. If there is a foreseeable disruption, schools should attempt to prevent its occurrence.

Disruptions do not need to be profound to justify student sanctioning. There is no need to wait for complete chaos, but there must be more than a mild distraction to the educational environment before schools may act. "There is no magic number of students or classrooms that need to be disturbed."[6] School administrators must be able to provide fact-intensive information about the disruption or the potential disruption before censorship of student expression is permissible. It is not sufficient that students merely talk about the offensive expressions or make general comments about the expressions. Likewise, expressions that make individuals self-conscious or uncomfortable do not justify censorship. However, schools may sanction a student if the expression realistically (1) depicts verbal or graphic violence, (2) threatens or undermines members of the school community, or (3) portends a violent disruption. Animated depictions of attacks on teachers are examples of graphic violence that may justify sanctioning of a student's expression. Undermining the professionalism of school administrators may justify sanctioning when it interferes with the effective operation of the school. Furthermore, most courts allow immediate sanctioning whenever a student makes comments analogous to "going Columbine." The dangers inherent in the school environment necessitate restricting speech threatening school shootings.

Some factors that need to be considered before censorship is permissible are

1. the record of past disturbance,
2. the number of individuals who viewed the expressions,

3. the location where the expressions were viewed or accessed,
4. the manner in which the expressions arrived on campus,
5. the student's intention that the expression impact the school environment, and
6. the necessity for supplementary administrative resources.

A significant connection between the student expression and the school must exist before administrative actions may be taken.

Rule 3: Censorship Is Permissible if the Student Expression Actually Interferes With Students' Rights to Educational Benefits or Substantially Detracts From the Learning Environment

Only expressions that actually impinge on the rights of other students may be censored. The courts do not allow school administrators to censor students' expression at all times, at all places, and under all circumstances. However, the courts do allow administrators to censor expression that inhibits a student from learning or experiencing educational benefits. If a student's expression attacks a core characteristic (race, ethnicity, disability, sexual orientation, or gender), then the expression may be censored if the expression did in fact interfere with a student's right to educational benefits or substantially detracts from the learning environment. Note that expressions that impinge on the rights of other students may be prohibited even when no substantial disruption to student activities is foreseeable.[7]

Rule 4: Lewd, Vulgar, or Profane Language Is Inappropriate in a Public Educational Environment

Schools have the authority to prohibit lewd, offensive, and vulgar student expressions from occurring on campus in public discourse.[8] Schools have the responsibility to prevent students from being subjected to language and material that is inappropriate for their physical and cognitive developmental level. The key factors are (1) the expression actually must occur on school campus and (2) expression must occur before a school audience. Cyber expressions created off campus may not be censored by the school, despite the offensiveness of such expressions. It is the parents' responsibility to monitor off-campus student expressions. Note that no substantial disruption needs to occur before a school may sanction based on this rule.

Rule 5: Reasonable Regulations May Be Imposed With Respect to the Time, Place, and Manner of Student Expressions Involving School Property, School Equipment, or School Events

Student expressions that are appropriate off campus or before some audiences are not always appropriate on school premises or before all students. Schools are not public forums; therefore, school administrators may impose reasonable restrictions of on-campus expressions created by students. Censorship is permissible if it is reasonably related to a pedagogical concern. Thus, schools may establish standards to prevent expressions that are ungrammatical, poorly written, inadequately researched, biased, or prejudiced, or that are expressed in an inappropriate tone. Schools must consider the emotional maturity of their populations in determining whether to disseminate student expressions on potentially sensitive topics. For example, schools may regulate dissemination of expressions that discuss the existence of Santa Claus in elementary schools or that present material that is inappropriate for an immature audience.

Rule 6: Schools May Regulate School-Sponsored Expression if the Expression Is Viewed as Endorsed by the Institution

School officials may more freely sanction school-sponsored expressions than student-initiated expressions. School-sponsored expressions include those created as part of the school curriculum or a school-sponsored activity. The school administrators exercise editorial control over student assignments, school publications, and other school-sponsored expressive activities. Therefore, schools may regulate expressions that bear "the imprimatur of the school."[9]

Rule 7: Schools May Regulate School-Sponsored Expression on the Basis of Any Legitimate Pedagogical Concern

Closely related to Rule 6 is this maxim that authorizes schools to censor student expression for legitimate pedagogical purposes. If there is a significant connection between the school and the student's expression, school administrators may exercise control. School administrators must accept that they may not intervene by sanctioning questionable expressions in cyber space that occur off campus during nonschool hours.

Rule 8: Off-Campus Expressions May Be Regulated Only When a Sufficient Nexus to Campus Is Shown

Only if the sting of the expression significantly impacts the school environment may the school intervene. The line is drawn where the expression disrupts school-related activities. Outside of that line, the school has no authority. For example, it is not the school's responsibility or necessarily within its authority to regulate all offensive or sexually suggestive photos posted on a student's social networking sites off campus and during summer break, if there is no reference or link to the school.[10] (Law enforcement and parents have authority over this conduct.) Conversely, it may be within the school's authority to sanction off-campus, online student expression when it violates a school's code of conduct. For example, online photos depicting student athletes drinking alcohol may warrant school administrative restrictions of extracurricular activities.[11] The distinguishing factor separating these two examples is the intimate connection between the campus and the student activity. The further the expression is attenuated from school activities, the less likely that the schools may moderate it.

Rule 9: Expression May Be Restricted if It Is Reasonably Perceived to Be Inconsistent With the "Shared Values of a Civilized Social Order"

School administrators have an affirmative obligation to instill in students the "fundamental values of 'habits and manners of civility' essential to democratic society" and to teach students "the boundaries of socially appropriate behavior."[12] Schools meet this obligation when they allow students to observe freedom of speech firsthand in order to see their constitutional rights at work. This does not mean that schools must allow students to advocate sex, drugs, or alcohol use in public educational institutions. Schools should impart boundaries for socially appropriate behavior.

Rule 10: True Threats and Criminal Activity May Always Be Regulated Regardless of Whether They Originated On or Off Campus

Schools may restrict student expression that falls outside of First Amendment protection, including true threats and criminal conduct. Additionally, schools need not tolerate activities that promote criminal conduct such as illegal drug use. The most difficult concept for school administrators to understand concerns true threats. Only the most egregious expressions fall within the definition of true threats. True threats must communicate a serious, unequivocal intent to harm someone or cause a reasonable person to feel immediately threatened. In today's society, most statements asserting school violence constitute true threats.

Conclusion

"Schools can and will adjust to the new challenges created by . . . students and the Internet, but not at the expense of the First Amendment."[13] Students need to know school boundaries exist, even on the Internet. By applying the **Top Ten Rules** suggested here, school administrators have a framework to assist them in enforcing appropriate boundaries dealing with student cyber expressions.

Notes

1. Hedges v. Wauconda Community School Dist. 118 9 F.3d 1295, 1297–1298 (7th Cir. 1993).
2. Bethel School District No. 403 v. Fraser, 478 U.S. 675, 683 (1986).
3. *Id.* at 681.
4. Vernonia Sch. Dist. 47J v. Acton (94-590), 515 U.S. 656 (1995).
5. Tinker v. Des Moines Independent Community School District, 393 U.S. 503, 508 (1969).

6. J.C. v. Beverly Hills Unified School District, 2010 LEXIS 54481, 44 (C.D. Cal. 2010).

7. Tinker, 515 U.S. at 509.

8. Bethel School District No. 403 v. Fraser, 478 U.S. 675, 681 (1986).

9. Hazelwood School District v. Kuhlmeier, 484 U.S. 260, 270–271 (1988).

10. Associated Press. (2009, November 3). *Ind. teens punished for racy MySpace photos sue high school.* Retrieved from http://www.firstamendmentcenter.org/news.aspx?id=22270.

11. Associated Press. (2008, January 11). *Facebook photos sting Minn. high school studies.* Retrieved from http://www.firstamendmentcenter.org/news.aspx?id=19537.

12. Bethel School District No. 403 v. Fraser, 478 U.S. 675, 681 (1986).

13. Hudson, D. (2008, August). *Cyberspeech.* First Amendment Center. Retrieved June 22, 2010, from http://www.firstamendmentcenter.org//speech/studentexpression/topic.aspx?topic=cyberspeech&SearchString=cyberspeech.

PART III

The MATRIX

An Administrator's Decision-Making Tool

12

Introduction to the MATRIX

School personnel frequently face the dilemma of where their school authority ends and their students' rights begin. The scenarios in this chapter—both from the Third Circuit Court of Appeals and both dated February 4, 2010—highlight this dilemma and raise the following questions:

- What should school administrators do when offensive student expression comes onto school property and disrupts school activities?
- How much disruption is necessary before school administrators may respond?
- Must the expression cause physical or emotional harm before sanctions may be imposed?
- Can vulgar or offensive expression always be censored by school administrators?
- Can schools step in and sanction the student who created the offensive expression?
- Do students have a constitutional right to express their controversial opinions with abandon?
- Does the fact that an expression was created off campus limit the school's authority to respond?
- May schools impose sanctions on student conduct that differ from the sanctions approved by the student's parent(s)?

The Problem: Example Scenarios

Scenario 1: Justin's Parody

Using his grandmother's computer, Justin, a 17-year-old honor student, created a parody profile of his principal on a social networking website. The profile contained a photo of the principal copied from the school's website. Justin posed interview questions and supplied answers that were supposedly from the principal. An example of Justin's questions and answers is below.[1]

Question	*Answer*
Are you a health freak?	big steroid freak
In the past month have you smoked?	big blunt
In the past month have you gone Skinny Dipping?	big lake not big dick
Ever been called a Tease?	big whore
Ever been Beaten up?	big fag
Interests?	Transgender, Appreciators of Alcoholic Beverages
Clubs you belong to:	Steroids International

Justin shared the profile with friends on the social networking site, and "word of the profile spread like wildfire and soon reached most, if not all, of Hickory High's student body."[2] Three other students created similar parodies of the principal, also on social networking sites, that were even more offensive and vulgar.

The principal learned about one of these parodies from his daughter. He was not happy. The principal reported the incident to the superintendent and asked the technology director to disable access to the profiles from school computers. Despite the directive, students still found ways to access the profiles. The principal himself soon found all four "degrading," "demeaning," "demoralizing," and "shocking" profiles.[3] Although not concerned for his safety, the principal contacted the police to discuss the possibility of filing harassment, defamation, and slander charges. No changes were ever filed.

Meanwhile, Justin accessed his social networking account in Spanish class and shared his parody profile with his classmates. In another class, a teacher briefly saw the principal's profile before telling the students to shut it down. Computer use was then limited to locations where students could be supervised, since the school was not able to completely block access to the social networking site.

Justin and his mother met with the school superintendent and school officials, and Justin confessed and apologized for creating the profile. After a hearing, Justin was given a 10-day out-of-school suspension, placed in an alternative education program, and banned from all extracurricular activities, including graduation. His parents grounded him and prohibited him from using the home computer. The parents sued the school district.

Scenario 2: J. S.'s Parody

Using her parents' home computer, J. S., a 14-year-old honor-roll student, created a parody profile of her principal on a social networking site. Her friend, K. L., added to the profile from her home computer as they communicated through AOL Instant Messenger. The profile contained the principal's photo, copied from the school's website. Although they did not identify the principal by name, the profile portrayed a middle-school principal. The parody posted questions and answers that included the following:[4]

Question	*Answer*
Interests	Being a tight ass, riding the Frain [name of guidance counselor] train, fucking in my office, hitting on children and their parents, "kidsrockmybed"
About Me	HELLO CHILDREN, yes. It's your oh-so-wonderful, hairy, expressionless, sex addict, fagass, put on this world with a small dick PRINCIPAL I have come to myspace so i can pervert the minds of other principals to be just like me. I know, I know, you're all thrilled . . .

The two girls initially set access to the profile as public, but soon changed it to private access. They granted "friend" status to 22 students. Since access to the social networking site was blocked at the middle school, the students had to view the site off campus.

A student informed the principal about the profile and its disturbing comments. The principal instructed the student to find out who created the profile and to bring him a printed copy of it. The student did both. Upon receiving a printout of the page, the principal was able to access the private profile. The principal was **not** happy. He reported the profile to the superintendent and the director of technology. They concluded that the profile violated the school's Acceptable Use Policy, because the photo was copied from the school's website. The principal did not believe that the site was a threat. He viewed it as an imposter profile and worried about its impact on the school and on his ability to adequately perform his duties as principal. The social networking site removed the profile upon the principal's request.

Two teachers quelled student discussions about the profile. A counselor proctored a test while administrators met with the parties involved. As a result, counseling appointments had to be rescheduled. After J. S. and K. L. were sanctioned and returned to school, two students decorated the girls' lockers. Those two students were sanctioned for that action, but the 20 to 30 students who congregated at the lockers were merely reprimanded. General disruption and rumblings broke out in several other classrooms, requiring teachers to respond. A few eighth-grade girls mentioned their concern to a teacher about the profile and its commentary concerning the principal and his family. The principal testified that there was "a severe deterioration of discipline at the Middle School . . . following the creation of the profile, his corresponding discipline of J. S. and K. L., and . . . the filing of the lawsuit" (p. 13).[5] The principal also reported stress-related health problems as a result of the incident.

Both girls admitted to creating the profile and apologized for their actions. The principal met with their parents. He gave J. S. and K. L. 10-day suspensions and prohibited them from attending school functions. The superintendent supported the sanctions. The police summoned the girls and their parents to the station to discuss the incident. Although the principal considered taking legal action, criminal harassment charges were not pursued based upon advice from the state police.

The facts of these two scenarios are remarkably similar. The court, however, reached different conclusions as to the appropriateness of the school's responses. Neither court case concluded that the vulgarity of the expression itself permitted a school to sanction the offending students. The Supreme Court has never applied the *Fraser* decision to conduct off school grounds. Under *Fraser*, student speech is not considered on-campus speech simply because it targets principals, students, or other members of the school community, even if it is reasonably foreseeable that the speech will make itself onto the campus. Territoriality is not necessarily the determining factor in limiting a school's authority to discipline students. Students may be disciplined, though, if their conduct poses a significant risk of substantial disruption at the educational institution. The ruling in these cases came down to whether or not a substantial risk of disruption occurred or was about to occur at the school.

In both scenarios, the speech was undoubtedly offensive; however, in Scenario 1 the speech was not satisfactorily proven to have impacted the school environment. Although the statements were personal and hurtful, there was no nexus shown between the inappropriate expressions and their effect upon the management and operations of the school. The statements were not shown to undermine the principal's fitness to serve in his official capacity. In contrast, the nexus was shown in Scenario 2. The effect of the speech was to explicitly and seriously undermine the operations and management of the school. The nexus between the website and its offensive comments was significant enough to cause the courts to find that it caused disruption in the school, health problems of the principal, adjustments to schedules, and interruptions to the academic mission of the school.

Distinguishing Characteristics

In Scenario 1, the court held "the school district failed to establish that a sufficient nexus existed between the student's creation and distribution of the profile and the school district, so that the district was permitted to regulate the students' conduct."[6]

Justin's parody did not sufficiently disrupt the school environment because

- No classes were canceled.
- The parody did not disrupt any teaching responsibilities or delivery of instruction.

- The vulgar statements, in and of themselves, did not undermine the principal's ability to perform his duties. The statements impugned the principal's personal reputation but not his professional reputation.
- Minimum time was spent controlling student reactions to the parody.
- Few additional resources or tasks were utilized in resolving the matter.
- No similar or past incidents had occurred to portend the viability of a substantial disruption.
- No physical or emotional repercussions were reported.
- The parody did not threaten any violence or encourage any act of violence.
- The parody expressed an opinion without calling for a response or reaction.

These two cases demonstrate the importance of documenting and differentiating the presenting conduct and the events surrounding a situation. School officials must be cognizant of how the presenting conduct connects to the school's environment. School officials must also be cautious in their sanctions so as to not interfere with parental rights. Decisions must also reflect community standards and be reasonably based on the totality of the circumstances. These complexities necessitate a management tool for school officials to use in weaving through the maze of decisions, communications, and emotions surrounding incidents of offensive expression. The MATRIX is that management tool.

The MATRIX offers practical, measured, and consistent solutions to school administrators and personnel for handling cyber bullying situations. It calculates the level of severity of the presenting conduct, reflects the culpability and characteristics of the offender, and considers the effect of the electronic aggression on the victims and the institutions.

The resulting score gives educators a numerical basis for leveling appropriate sanctions. The sanctions could include, but are not limited to, legal referrals, expulsion, suspension, detention, warnings, extracurricular restrictions, and discussions. The intermediate MATRIX calculations provide insight into areas that the school system might ultimately pursue. Those areas include counseling for the offender and victims, psychosocial intervention programs, anger management lessons, educational programs, and rehabilitation services to redress problematic circumstances.

Philosophical Goals

The primary purpose of the MATRIX is to provide a uniform, objective foundation for a school's response to cyber aggression. The guidelines generated by the MATRIX will reduce unwarranted disparity (race, gender, socioeconomic, etc.) and retain administrative discretion. To that end, the School Sanctioning Worksheet has been created to identify the predominant objective factors that are relevant in analyzing the situation and prescribing the disposition. The worksheet evaluates the offender's personal background, prior disciplinary record, and role in the offense.

Aggravating factors are weighed against mitigating factors. Distinctions between the individual characteristics of the child offender, the types of offending conduct, and the conduct's impact on the victim(s), school, and society are also considered. Basically, the MATRIX balances the score of the presenting offense plus the offender's personal score against mitigating factors surrounding the offender and concomitant circumstances. The total score reflects the need for and the level of the sanction that is appropriate for the offense.

A secondary outcome resulting from the use of the MATRIX's School Sanctioning Worksheet is that it provides documentation supporting the school's decision. This documentation includes weighted scores that evaluate details about the presenting conduct and about the characteristics of the offender and victim(s). The documentation also reports information verifying if and when parents and/or legal authorities are contacted. The factors listed on the worksheet serve as guidelines but are not all inclusive.

Another outcome is that the MATRIX serves as a predictive philosophical tool, highlighting important facets of the disposition phase for inappropriate cyber conduct. The worksheet promotes transparent accountability and assists the stakeholders (offenders, victims, bystanders, and school administrators) in understanding the sanctioning process. The worksheet provides notification to all stakeholders and defines what conduct is inappropriate and which behaviors or actions will increase or decrease the sanctions.

Uniformity and consistency are important in disciplinary situations involving juveniles; however, flexibility is equally significant. The MATRIX addresses these goals by promoting similarity of sanctioning in an area that was heretofore unstructured. The MATRIX also allows for flexibility by taking into consideration the unique characteristics of the offender. The resulting sanctions should be uniform across jurisdictions and proportionate to the level of the presenting conduct. Sanctioning should be unbiased, yet reflect the culpability of the offender, the effect on the victim(s), and the treatment needed to remedy the underlying problem or prevent it from recurring.

The MATRIX Tool

The MATRIX is a practical, decision-making tool for addressing cyber bullying situations by school administrators. The MATRIX

- Objectively standardizes aggravating and mitigating circumstances.
- Provides summary documentation to support the school administration's disciplinary decision.
- Establishes a uniform benchmark for evaluating similar cyber bullying situations.
- Offers transparency in the sanctioning process.

School administrators are no longer isolated in the decision-making process. With widespread use, the MATRIX will allow administrators to model and conform their disciplinary decisions to those used by other school officials confronted with comparable incidents. The MATRIX was designed to provide transparent and systematic accountability for the variability in offenders and in offenses surrounding cyber bullying. The School Sanctioning Worksheet summarizes explicit sanctioning considerations and supporting context for the decision-making process.

CAVEAT

The MATRIX provides an objective framework within which to structure a sanctioning decision. It does not dictate specific sanctions and should be used as a guide only. The material in the MATRIX is advisory, and its use is voluntary. School administrators must consider what is an appropriate sanction based on community standards, policies of regional offices of education, and specific state legislative directives. The sanctioning considerations should be regularly reviewed for viability and revision appropriate to specific school districts. If any discrepancies arise between school or state policies and the book's recommendations, always defer to independent legal counsel. Decisions to act or refrain from acting should not be determined on the basis of this information without seeking legal advice. The MATRIX is intended to complement a school district's preexisting decision-making practices, not to replace them.

Notes

1. Layshock v. Hermitage School District, 593 F.3d 249, 252 (3d Cir. 2010).
2. *Id.* at 253.
3. *Id.*
4. J.S. et al. v. Blue Mountain School District, 593 F.3d 286, 291 (3d Cir. 2010), *vacated, rehearing en banc* (pending 6/3/2010), 2010 LEXIS 7342 (3d Cir. Apr. 9, 2010).
5. J.S. et al., 593 F.3d at 294.
6. *Id.* at 302.

13

Working the MATRIX

The MATRIX is a comprehensive assessment tool for objectively processing a cyber bullying incident involving a school institution. The MATRIX applies whenever a reported incident of suspected cyber aggression occurs. The purpose of the MATRIX is not to respond to the immediacy of the situation; rather, the MATRIX provides guidance supporting the sanctions that school administrators ultimately assign to the offending student.

The MATRIX is composed of six sections:

Section 1: Status and personal characteristics from the student/offender's school records and general background contact information on those involved in the incident.

Section 2: The category and description of the presenting conduct.

Section 3: Numerical calculations correlating to the intensity of the presenting offense.

Section 4: Numerical calculations correlating to the offender's status and personal characteristics.

Section 5: Numerical calculations mitigating the offender's liability for his or her conduct.

Section 6: The total sanctioning score and actual disposition received.

The MATRIX: School Sanctioning Worksheet

Figure 13.1 displays the six sections presented on the School Sanctioning Worksheet. The worksheet can also be found at the back of the book and in electronic form at www.corwin.com/cyberbullying.

Figure 13.1 School Sanctioning Worksheet

Cyber Bullying MATRIX: School Sanctioning Worksheet©	**Student Name** Last: First: Middle:	Date of Birth (DOB): Phone Number:	Sex:
	Parent/Guardian:	Phone Number:	Grade Level:
	Parent/Guardian:	Phone Number:	School District Number:
	Legal Representative:	Phone Number:	

Offender—Date(s) Contacted/Summary:			
Parent(s)—Date(s) Contacted/Summary:			
Legal Rep(s)—Date(s) Contacted/Summary:			
Victim 1—Date(s) Contacted/Summary:	DOB:	Sex:	Grade Level:

Presenting Conduct	Date and Explanation
A. Criminal Civil Conduct Outside First Amendment Protection	
B. Acceptable Use Policy (AUP) Violation(s)	
C. Substantial Material Disruptions	
D. Interference With Rights of Others (including Title IX, ADA)	
E. Lewd/Vulgar/Indecent/Plainly Offensive Speech	
F. Anti–Legitimate Pedagogical Concerns (school's imprimatur)	
G. Anti–Social Civic Values	
H. Netiquette Violations (protected by First Amendment)	

Presenting Offense Score								Offender Score								Mitigation Score							
A	Seriousness Category	0	1	2	3	4	5	A	Leader Follower	0	1	2	3	4	5	A	Offender Age	0	1	2	3	4	5
B	Vicious/Heinous Conduct	0	1	2	3	4	5	B	Active/Passive Participation	0	1	2	3	4	5	B	Cognitive/Physical Development	0	1	2	3	4	5

(Continued)

Figure 13.1 (Continued)

C	Duration	0	1	2	3	4	5	C	Obstructionist's Activities	0	1	2	3	4	5	C	Voluntarily Seeking Treatment	0	1	2	3	4	5
D	Number of Victims	0	1	2	3	4	5	D	Exploiting Positions of Trust	0	1	2	3	4	5	D	Issue Already Being Addressed	0	1	2	3	4	5
E	Victim Injury Level	0	1	2	3	4	5	E	Current Supervision	0	1	2	3	4	5	E	Admission of Guilt	0	1	2	3	4	5
F	Victim Vulnerability	0	1	2	3	4	5	F	Prior Disciplinary Actions	0	1	2	3	4	5	F	Cooperation/Atonement	0	1	2	3	4	5
G	Gang Involvement	0	1	2	3	4	5	G	Lack of School Participation	0	1	2	3	4	5	G	Restitution	0	1	2	3	4	5
H	Under the Influence	0	1	2	3	4	5	H	School/Student Nexus	0	1	2	3	4	5	H	Current Behavior	0	1	2	3	4	5
I	Multiple Violations	0	1–5	1–5	1–5	1–5	1–5	I	School/Conduct Nexus	0	1	2	3	4	5	I	Victim's Role in Offense	0	1	2	3	4	5
J	Other	0	1	2	3	4	5	J	Other	0	1	2	3	4	5	J	Other	0	1	2	3	4	5
		Total =								Total =								Total =					

Presenting Offense Score	+	Offender Score	–	Mitigation Score	= ___________ Total	
Date and Description of Actual Disposition Imposed:					Worksheet Prepared By:	

Caveat

The MATRIX provides an objective framework within which to structure a sanctioning decision. It does not dictate specific sanctions and should be used as a guide only. **The MATRIX is advisory, and its use is voluntary.** School administrators must consider what is an appropriate sanction based on community standards, the policies of regional offices of education, and specific state legislative directives. If any discrepancies arise between school or state policies and the manual's recommendations, always defer to independent legal counsel. Decisions to act or refrain from acting should not be determined on the basis of this information without seeking legal advice. **The MATRIX is intended to complement a school district's preexisting decision-making practices, not to replace them.**

Section 1: Student Offender and Background Information

The first section contains the student *offender's* background information and general contact information relative to those involved with the cyber bullying incident. This section should accurately document the student's name, age, date of birth, sex, and grade level. This section also requires all contact information relevant to the administrator's meetings or discussions with the student, including acknowledgment if a parent, guardian, or legal representative was present. (If the child has legal representation, it is always prudent to keep the school's legal counsel informed of the situation.) When meetings or contacts occur with the child and/or his representatives, a summary of each session should be duly noted on the worksheet. Each summary should contain, at a minimum, the date, those in attendance, and the results of that session, including recommendations, reprimands, and referrals. See Figure 13.2.

This section also requires documentation regarding the school administrator's contact with any and all *victim*(s). Specifically, this section requires that the administrator record the names of victim(s) and their representatives who made contact with the school regarding the cyber incident. Included on the worksheet should be a listing of all who were present during the contact and a summary of the date

Figure 13.2 Student Offender and Background Information

<table>
<tr><td rowspan="4">Cyber Bullying MATRIX: School Sanctioning Worksheet©</td><td>Student Name
Last: First: Middle:</td><td>Date of Birth (DOB):
Phone Number:</td><td>Sex:</td></tr>
<tr><td>Parent/Guardian:</td><td>Phone Number:</td><td>Grade Level:</td></tr>
<tr><td>Parent/Guardian:</td><td>Phone Number:</td><td rowspan="2">School District Number:</td></tr>
<tr><td>Legal Representative:</td><td>Phone Number:</td></tr>
<tr><td colspan="4">Offender—Date(s) Contacted/Summary:</td></tr>
<tr><td colspan="4">Parent(s)—Date(s) Contacted/Summary:</td></tr>
<tr><td colspan="4">Legal Rep(s)—Date(s) Contacted/Summary:</td></tr>
<tr><td colspan="4">Victim 1—Date(s) Contacted/Summary: DOB: Sex: Grade Level:</td></tr>
</table>

and substance of the meeting. Further, if any recommendations, reprimands, or referrals were made, those too should be noted. If more than one victim was contacted, each should be documented and included as a supplement to the form. (Again, if a victim has legal representation, it is always prudent to keep the school's legal counsel informed of the situation.)

This background documentation should contain any information that may be relevant to the unique characteristics of the student offender or the victim(s). For example, if the offender has a history of violent behaviors, suicidal tendencies, or emotional concerns, this information should be noted, as it is necessary to justify emergency expulsions or sanctions. It should also be noted that all **documentation should be constantly updated to reflect the current status of the student(s).**[1]

Additional documentation should be made if a victim has special needs, has been previously victimized, or is targeted based on individual attributes (e.g., personality characteristics, physical attributes, ethnicity, race, or sexual orientation).

Generally schools have no duty to protect students from peer-on-peer harm. This is true even when the school is aware of potentially harmful situations, as was the case in the Columbine massacre. Compulsory school attendance does not create a custodial special relationship such that schools have an obligatory duty to protect. Schools are typically immune from this tort liability based on the Eleventh Amendment. However, schools may have a duty to protect if the harm is systemic and affects a student's ability to receive an education or detracts from the learning environment.

Several recent lawsuits alleging peer-on-peer bullying harassment have supported viable causes of actions. Gender-related harassment lawsuits under Title IX have caused schools to be financially liable. Likewise, disability lawsuits may also provide relief to victims. If a school has actual knowledge of the abuse and provides no remedial relief, or if the remedial efforts are ineffective time after time, schools may be liable. Schools cannot overlook chronic bullying. Schools must engage in a concerted effort to stop systemic bullying. Reviewing a school's MATRIX documentation would alert the school of systemic problems and the efforts used to address the issues.

If a school district can provide evidence through documentation or example that it attempted to rectify the abusive situations, it may be saved from liability. In *Yap v. Oceanside Union Free School District*,[2] the court found in favor of a school district because it "doggedly, but unsuccessfully attempted to address" the Yaps' allegations of bullying and harassment."[3] In *Yap,* the principal documented each bullying incident, investigated it, and admonished the bullies. She also invoked schoolwide tolerance education, denied recess and lunch privileges, and created an antibullying curriculum, all to no avail; the bullying continued. However, because the principal had instituted and **documented a variety of measures** used to deter the bullying, she avoided liability.

The MATRIX worksheet documentation assists schools in meeting their burden of showing reasonable steps to address cyber bullying. Completion of the MATRIX worksheet for each incident will enable the school to see the **longitudinal picture of the victimization** of students. Completion of the worksheet will also provide documentation on the variety of techniques used to stop the bullying. Using the MATRIX worksheet, school administrators easily will be able to view the overall picture of the cyber bullying problem and the solutions that have been attempted. Administrators can see the "forest and the trees" and limit future liability issues.

Section 2: Presenting Conduct

Figure 13.3 Presenting Conduct

Presenting Conduct	Date and Explanation
A. Criminal Civil Conduct Outside First Amendment Protection	
B. Acceptable Use Policy (AUP) Violation(s)	
C. Substantial Material Disruptions	
D. Interference With Rights of Others (including Title IX, ADA)	
E. Lewd/Vulgar/Indecent/Plainly Offensive Speech	
F. Anti–Legitimate Pedagogical Concerns (school's imprimatur)	
G. Anti–Social Civic Values	
H. Netiquette Violations (protected by First Amendment)	

Presenting conduct refers to the categories of cyber bullying conduct corresponding to criminal offenses or legal precedent. The following eight categories of expressive conduct are of concern to school authorities.

A. *Criminal and civil conduct that is outside First Amendment protection.* True threats, obscenity, sexting, defamation, and fighting words are included in this category.

B. *Acceptable use policy (AUP) violation(s).* Schools have established contracts with students and their parents related to use of technology in the school. Sanctions may occur if students violate these policies.

C. *Substantial and material disruption of the educational institution.* Student expressions that create or forecast adverse reactions on school premises are included in this category. Schools do not need to wait for the actual disruption to occur before acting.

D. *Interference with others.* Student expression may be sanctioned when it seriously infringes on the ability of other students to get an education or detracts from the learning environment.

E. *Lewd, vulgar, indecent, and plainly offensive speech.* Schools may regulate improper speech that offends the sensibilities of children due to their age and cognitive development level only if the expression occurs on school premises. Vulgar speech occurring off campus may not be regulated. Parents must supervise the expressions of their children that occur beyond the schoolyard gates.

F. *Anti–legitimate pedagogical concerns.* School officials may censor school-sponsored student expression for valid content-neutral educational reasons. Schools maintain control over expressions that bear the imprimatur of the school or expressions that are viewed as the school's own speech.

G. *Anti–social civic values.* School officials may sanction expression that encourages illegal drug use. Schools teach the habits and manners of civility as well as fundamental values.

H. *Netiquette violations.* Schools may not sanction netiquette violations. Rude and immature expressions may be hurtful, but they are protected by the First Amendment. Schools should educate the student audience rather than squelch student speech.

Category A: Criminal and Civil Conduct That Is Outside First Amendment Protection

Threats

True threats occur when "a reasonable person would foresee that the statement would be interpreted by those to whom the maker communicates the statement as a serious expression of intent to harm or assault."[4] If a true threat occurs, school administrators may always sanction the conduct. Generally true threats occur in face-to-face situations, but there are some exceptions. True threats over the Internet are rare.

Schools face many situations that involve threatening expressions, but few are classified as true threats. However, post *Morse,* courts allow schools to intervene and sanction students for grave threatening expressions. Post Columbine, the courts have taken physical threats of violence seriously and authorize sanctioning without a *Tinker* analysis. Sanctioning is permissible due to the nature of the school environment. Just as schools were allowed to censor Morse's drug expression (Bong Hits 4 Jesus), they may also censor serious expressions of violence against students or school personnel.

Sexting

Criminal behavior such as sexting is emerging as a more frequent technology-based activity involving students. Sexting refers to the sending or posting of sexually suggestive material, primarily pictures, over the phone or the Internet. This activity is illegal, and the conduct falls within child pornography legislation. If convicted, child offenders must register as sex offenders and face harsh punishments. Legislatures are exploring calibrated responses to downgrade the punishment or lessen the severity of the offense if committed by juveniles.

School authorities should carefully consider whether or not to refer sexting matters to law enforcement authorities. Criminal prosecution of children is considered a root cause encouraging the "school-to-prison pipeline." This theory supports the belief that students who are prosecuted are funneled on a path toward prison. These students eventually wind up in the "criminal justice system, where prison is the end of the road."[5]

Schools should not support a zero-tolerance policy whereby all sexting is referred to law enforcement authorities. Consequences result in students missing more school, because they are punished both at the school and through the juvenile court. "Studies have shown that a child who has been suspended is more likely to be retained in grade, to drop out, to commit a crime, and/or to end up incarcerated as an adult."[6] While zero tolerance policies provide schools with a convenient approach to deal with certain situations, a school should not abdicate its disciplinary responsibility to law enforcement or juvenile authorities. Schools should, at a minimum, educate students as to the proper use of technology and online resources. For example, students should be taught that taking promiscuous photos of themselves or others is inappropriate. Because **sexting is a criminal activity, schools have the absolute authority to censor it.** Sexting is not First Amendment protected expression.

Fighting Words

Another exception to the free speech protection of students concerns fighting words. **Fighting words** can be regulated if the words intentionally provoke a given group to immediately react in a hostile manner. No cases were found that dealt directly with this category of unprotected speech on school premises. In school cases, analogous to fighting words are expressions intentionally provoking reasonable fear or apprehension on the part of the audience. **The expression** (spoken and written words, communicative actions) **must be made in a school setting** and **gravely threaten violence** to the school's population. The *Boim* case previously discussed exemplifies this point. In *Boim,* a student wrote a first person fictional piece, titled "Dream," wherein she described the shooting of her sixth period math teacher. The court allowed Rachel to be sanctioned, because her fictional piece was created on school premises. She was **not** sanctioned for the content of her essay. She was sanctioned because she had expressed herself at school. The court concluded there was no First Amendment right to express comments reasonably perceived as threats in a school environment. Just as one is not allowed to yell "fire" in a theater or make "bomb" references in an airport, students may not make grave threats reasonably perceived as violent in a school.

Category B: Acceptable Use Policy (AUP) Violation(s)

Student handbooks usually contain contracts (AUPs) related to the use of technology for students and their parents. Disciplinary sanctions can occur if students violate these policies. Schools may entirely ban cell phones or restrict access to personal websites during the school day. Such conduct would not run afoul of the First Amendment. Such measures would be permissible content-neutral time, place, and manner regulations. Under First Amendment jurisprudence,

> The principal inquiry in determining content neutrality, in speech cases generally and in time, place, or manner cases in particular, is whether the government has adopted a regulation of speech because of disagreement with the message it conveys [citation omitted]. The government's purpose is the controlling consideration. A regulation that serves purposes unrelated to the content of expression is deemed neutral, even if it has an incidental effect on some speakers or messages but not others.[7]

A total ban of student use of technology is content neutral and a reasonable time, place, and manner restriction. The problem with a total ban policy is that students creatively find methods of circumventing it. Another issue focuses on the schools' responsibility to teach students to function in today's society. Students need to learn appropriate and responsible use of technology and the Internet.

Schools cannot have overly broad policies to limit school expression, nor may they have policies that ban derogatory comments that refer to race, ethnic differences, religion, sexual orientation, or disability; such policies are unconstitutional. Schools do not have the legal right to prevent criticism of beliefs or a way of life.[8]

AUPs have to be narrowly defined, reasonable, and designed to further the mission of the school. They must also be flexible enough to accommodate a number of different school situations. As Justice Alito said, "No court or legislature has ever suggested that unwelcome speech directed at another's values may be prohibited under the rubric of anti-discrimination."[9] Anti–racial harassment policies that prohibit certain categories of activities are permissible, if the category is sufficiently related to actual instances of previous disturbances. General categories prohibiting expressions that create ill will are too vague. For example, the Jeff Foxworthy t-shirt case[10] and the rosary case[11] were too vague, while the Confederate flag cases were acceptable.

Category C: Substantial and Material Disruption

In limited situations, schools are given additional authority to control student expressions that impact the educational environment. These situations are limited and strictly defined by court precedent. They were discussed ad nauseam in Chapter 2.

1. Was there an actual and substantial disruption of the educational environment?
2. Was the expression itself sufficiently violent or threatening to members of the school so as to automatically portend violent disruption?
3. What is the school's record of similar past disruption?
4. Did it truly disrupt administrative practices?
5. Was the disciplinary decision based on objective facts or on a subjective emotional reaction to the expression itself?

A student expression may be controlled if it **substantially disrupts the school environment or the educational process.** Justice Alito believes that schools must have the authority to intervene "before speech leads to violence."[12] Specific fear of or an actual disruption is required, not just some remote apprehension or possibility of a disturbance.

Since the Columbine shootings, courts rarely interfere with schools punishing expression that contains threatening elements. However, there seems to be a distinction within the case law between when the threats are aimed at students and when the threats are aimed at school administrators and faculty. If the threat is against a child, courts are more likely to uphold a school's sanctions.

Category D: Interference With the Rights of Others

Peer-on-peer harassment imposes liability on the school only when it is subjectively and objectively severe or extensive enough that it limits or denies a student's participation in or benefit from an educational program. Schools are entitled to restrict any speech that undermines a student's right to learn or administrators' ability to professionally carry out their duties.

Category E: Lewd, Vulgar, Indecent, and Plainly Offensive Speech

Schools may limit lewd, indecent, or offensive speech for the same reasons that obscenity is a crime. The *Hazelwood* Court defined indecent speech as speech that is ungrammatical, poorly written, biased, vulgar, or "unsuitable for immature audiences."[13] A school has to be able to set high standards for student speech that is disseminated under its auspices. These standards can be higher than those used by newspaper publishers or producers in the real world. Schools as instruments of the state must provide lessons of civility that are age appropriate. Schools have the duty to nurture civility and educate the young for citizenship, so deference will be given to school officials to promote socially appropriate behavior.[14]

The precedent provided by *Fraser* is limited to lewd, vulgar, indecent, and plainly offensive comments. Vulgar and lewd speech undermines a school's educational mission. Limiting these types of speech involves teaching appropriate forms and manners of speech—not its content, substance, or viewpoint. Schools cannot discipline a student for a political viewpoint, but they can discipline for a sexually explicit speech in a school assembly.

Students are allowed to express their dissatisfaction with issues but must do so in a manner that is appropriate to a public school setting. Definitions of inappropriate expressions must be limited to the time, place, and manner in which students make the expressions. This category of offensive speech is typically applied when the expression itself occurs on campus. Schools generally do not have the authority to punish lewd and profane speech occurring off campus.

Category F: Anti-Legitimate Pedagogical Concerns

The *Hazelwood* Court stated that a school may curb "speech that is inconsistent with its basic educational mission."[15] Administrators may control speech in school-sponsored activities only if their controls are related to legitimate pedagogical concerns. These legitimate concerns include expressions that

- Communicate civic pride to students. [16]
- Establish socially appropriate boundaries for students.[17]
- Encourage civil, age-appropriate, mature conduct.[18]
- Demonstrate constitutional rights at work.
- Instruct students in proper grammar, spelling, and styles of expression.[19]

Under the category of legitimate pedagogical concerns, the school has the right to monitor any and all expressions that are reasonably viewed as the school's own speech, both on and off campus.[20] For example, if the perception is that the expression reflects the school's opinions, then the school has the authority to regulate the expression. School newspapers, websites, newsletters, and any other school-sponsored productions are also examples of expressions bearing the imprimatur of the school, and thus they may be regulated.[21]

"School 'sponsorship' of student speech is not lightly to be presumed."[22] School sponsorship occurs when the expression (1) involved school assignments or school-sponsored activity, (2) was created on school computers and/or used school resources, or (3) appeared to deliver opinions promoted by the school.

Category G: Anti-Social Civic Values

Schools may sanction and take steps to safeguard speech that can reasonably be regarded as encouraging illegal activity.[23] No showing of lewdness, obscenity, or vulgarity is necessary. Nor is any substantial disruption required. Schools may, because of their environment, prohibit expression that conflicts with their self-defined educational mission. For instance, expressions of opinions concerning drug usage may be appropriate in other settings but not in a public school.

In *Ponce*, E. P.'s writings were not sanctionable because they were vague. No specific threat was made to any particular student. Rather, the writings were sanctionable because a failure to sanction them would send a message to E. P. and others that the school administration would tolerate violent threats against the student body. The school was permitted to punish E. P., because the expressions contained in the notebook created a danger, like *Morse*'s drug expression, that "is far more serious and palpable"[24] than the dangers inherent in restricting free speech in school.

Category H: Netiquette Violations

Teasing and name calling among school children, even when they refer to gender differences, is **not** sanctionable.[25] Epithets, discourteous comments, and rudeness may not be sanctioned unless they are **so** pervasive that they substantially interfere with a student's ability to get an education. This approach is similar to the contours creating an objectively hostile or abusive work environment under Title VII of the Civil Rights Act of 1964.[26] Teasing and name calling are netiquette violations and should be handled by educating the speaker, not sanctioning the conduct.

Section 3: Presenting Offense Score

This section contains a rubric for assessing the seriousness of the presenting offense as identified under Section 2. The rubric includes 10 subsections, each rated on a **zero (0) through five (5)** scale. See Figure 13.4.

Figure 13.4 Presenting Offense Score

Presenting Offense Score								
A	Seriousness Category	0	1	2	3	4	5
B	Vicious/Heinous Conduct	0	1	2	3	4	5
C	Duration	0	1	2	3	4	5
D	Number of Victims	0	1	2	3	4	5
E	Victim Injury Level	0	1	2	3	4	5
F	Victim Vulnerability	0	1	2	3	4	5
G	Gang Involvement	0	1	2	3	4	5
H	Under the Influence	0	1	2	3	4	5
I	Multiple Violations	0	1–5	1–5	1–5	1–5	1–5
J	Other	0	1	2	3	4	5
		Total =					

Each of the categories A-J is explained here.

Category A: Seriousness Category

This category addresses the seriousness or level of **intensity** of the presenting conduct.

- Was the offense one in which serious outcomes could be expected? (Or was it, in contrast, an anomaly, unlikely to reoccur or cause serious outcomes?)
- What long-term impact does or did the incident have on the school or individuals?
- How many resources (time, personnel, money) did the school employ to "fix" the situation or circumstance?
- What is the impact of the action(s) on the school as a whole?

The more resounding the "yes" provided for the first question, and the stronger the assertions used to answer the others, the greater the number of points that should be allocated to this offense. If students suggest in their expression(s) that they are going to "go Columbine," they would receive 5 points. This is because they have explicitly stated an intention to commit a serious offense by making an in-person threat to harm a particular student, administrator, teacher, or other staff member. Even if they did not have any intentions of following through on the statement, the statement alone causes serious repercussions.

Another example would include tampering with the school's technology or website so that experts must be employed to repair the damage. Seriousness involves significant harm or disruption to a particular person or to the institution.

An offense is less serious when a student creates a website that is predominantly personal but that includes a statement or two attacking the job performance of a school administrator. Such an offense would be allocated 0 points or 1 point. A 0 or a 1 would also be appropriate when a student's website informs the world that a coach plays only his or her favorites, not those who are skilled and talented. Both of these are so low that unless there is a substantial disruption to school functioning, neither warrants sanctioning. However, if a student's attack of a school administrator's job performance goes to the heart of and administrator's ability to performance his or her job, more points should be allocated. For example, when the student insinuates that the principal is having sex with his students, that offense should be allocated 4 or 5 points.

Heightened vulgarity used in relation to the age, maturity, and cognitive development of the audience should rate a somewhat serious response. For example, in *Fraser,* where the student speaker made sexual innuendos at an all-school assembly before 600 students, the offense would garner a midlevel rubric score—perhaps a 3. This rating would result from the subjection of the younger students to age-inappropriate crude and lewd statements.

Category B: Vicious/Heinous Conduct

This category allows for weighted consideration due to extreme nastiness of a student's expression: crimes that involve significant injury or hate crimes. The two cases involving student-created videos show the extremes. In *Requa v. Kent School District No. 415,*[27] the student created a webpage mocking his teacher by making references to her "booty" and her lack of organizational skills. This webpage was disruptive and upsetting to the teacher; however, it would garner only 1 or maybe 2 points. This website was more of an embarrassment than a vicious attack. On the other hand, in *O.Z. v. Board of Trustees of Long Beach Unified School District,* [28] where the student created a video depicting a butcher knife lunging at the teacher, the offense would garner a possible 4 or 5 points. The intensity of the violent images and really vulgar language made O. Z.'s video more heinous. The higher point allocations are reserved for expressions that are extremely cruel or degrading toward specific individuals.

Category C: Duration

This category involves expressions that continue over time or are amplified by mass distribution. It also includes expressions that involve a persistent course of conduct. An additional aspect to duration encompasses frequency. In *J.C. v. Beverly Hills Unified School District,*[29] the student's website was accessed 90 times. If the expressions ("slut," "ugliest piece of shit") were deemed worthy of suppression, the duration score would be significant—a 3 or a 4.

Another example would be the case of *Doninger v. Niehoff.*[30] In *Doninger,* the student placed an announcement on an open blog encouraging responses to her criticism of the school's postponement of a musical event. After the announcement went out, the school was inundated with phone calls and e-mails. The school was required to devote excessive amounts of time and manpower responding. The student's expression was of sufficient duration or involved such frequency that it would rate a score of 3.

A score of 5 is reserved for those cases wherein the abusive expressions continued over time. In *L.W. v. Toms River Regional Schools,*[31] L. W. was physically abused and called "faggot," "homo," and "butt boy" by other students on a daily basis over a period of four years. Likewise, in *Lowery v. Euverard,*[32] the Michigan student endured repeated attacks from sixth to ninth grade. The incidents included over 200 occasions of name calling ("queer," "fagot," "pig," "Mr. Clean") in seventh grade alone. He also endured numerous other attacks; students shoved him into a school locker, urinated on his clothes, and mocked him in classes. The attacks escalated from words to a sexual assault. Both of these cases would clearly suggest a score of 5.

Category D: Number of Victims

In this category, attention is given to the number of individuals victimized by the expression(s). *Victim,* as defined here, includes the bullied individual(s) as well as bystanders affected by the activity(ies). For example, attacks made against the entire school or a group within the school—such as those at Columbine—fall within this ambit. Often, this may include innocent bystanders who became disturbed in the aftermath of the incident(s). This will include individuals (students and adults) who need counseling, supportive changes in their lives, and accommodations from home and/or school. This will also include the groups of individuals (e.g., intellectuals, techno-smart, nonathletic, racially diverse, special needs, or just different) who are ostracized. **The greater the number of victims, the higher the score.**

Category E: Victim Injury Level

The more serious the victim's injury, the higher the given numerical score will be.

- Did the victim suffer long- or short-term injuries?
- Did the victim suffer from permanent injuries or commit suicide?
- Did the victim lose a significant or a minor amount of instructional time?
- Was the victim forced to make a major life adjustment—such as relocate, change schools, and so forth?

As a result of being sexually attacked in the locker room by a teammate, Lowery received extensive injuries both physically and emotionally. The extent of his injuries would result in a score of 5. Likewise, when cyber bullying results in a victim's suicide, need for intensive counseling, or inability to work at all, the score should be a 5. The inability to work for a time or short-term hospitalizations or treatments would be scored from 2 to 4, depending upon the degree or level of loss.

In *J.S. ex rel. H.S. v. Bethlehem Area School District,*[33] the teacher suffered extreme distress after learning of the posting involving her head dripping in blood and the recruitment of a hitman. She testified that she suffered extreme symptoms of stress anxiety. This resulted in losses of appetite, sleep, and weight. She also suffered headaches, took antianxiety/antidepressant medication, feared leaving her home, and crowds. This would score as a 5.

A score of a 0 or 1 would result in a case such as *Klein v. Smith.*[34] Therein the student gave "the finger" to a school authority figure. Although upsetting and disrespectful, the gesture caused little to no harm to the victim.

Category F: Victim Vulnerability

This category covers the degree to which the victim was vulnerable to attack when the offender was aware of the vulnerability. Individuals viewed as vulnerable include those with special needs and those who are young, physically limited, or emotionally/psychologically challenged or impaired. It also includes those of a different size from the offender and those with different physical attributes, as well as those with minority group status due to their race, religion, or sexual preferences. The question that should be asked is, Did the offender take advantage of any vulnerability or disability?

Age span between the offender and victim is also a consideration. The greater the age span between the older offender and the younger victim, the higher the score should be.

If the offender is aware of a vulnerability regarding the victim's emotional history, this might also increase the number of points. Attacking these individuals garners higher scores. For example, posting a sexually explicit photo depicting a special needs student on a website would result in a score of 2, whereas posting emotionally charged materials, **knowing that the victim suffers low self-esteem or psychological problems and intending** to cause suicidal ideation or to result in emotional distress, would rate a 5.

Category G: Gang Involvement

If the offender is involved with a gang or group of any type (formal or informal), and if the offense furthers the gang's agenda to destroy, hurt, or ostracize another individual or group, a number of points will be assigned. The degree to which the expression was encouraged through gang activity will identify the number of points. A score of 0 will be assessed when **no** gang involvement exits. A score of 1 would be assigned in a case like *Chalifoux v. New Caney Independent School District.*[35] If that school district had shown that the girls were gang members and that their display of the rosary beads was an expression of gang solidarity, then the activity would qualify for 1 point.

The case of *Sypniewski v. Warrant Hills Regional Board of Education*[36] exemplifies where higher scores would result. In *Sypniewski,* the school district provided evidence of pervasive racial disturbances associated with a gang known as "the Hicks." Members of this group expressed themselves in a number of inappropriate ways: A white student arrived at school with a black face and a rope tied in a noose around his neck, members dressed in clothing bearing the Confederate flag, and members observed "White Power Wednesdays" by wearing Confederate flag clothing.[37] These student expressions resulted in an interracial fight where one student sustained a concussion and required stitches.[38] These expressions involving the gang apparel (Confederate flag) would result in a score of 3, 4, or 5.

Category H: Under the Influence

If student expressions are made while under the influence of alcohol or illegal substances, this would result in the addition of points. The greater the influence of the substance on the activity, the greater the number of points assigned. Substance abuse is a choice. Thus, being under the influence is not an excuse when a student commits an offense. It is an aggravating condition.

Category I: Multiple Violations

Students may engage in multiple inappropriate activities at the same time. In *O. Z.*, for example the student violated the school's AUPs by video recording his teacher during class. The video was threatening and disruptive to the school environment, and it contained inappropriate and vulgar language ("bitch," "fat bastard"). Potentially, *O. Z.* committed three violations. If each were sustained (founded), the offense score should reflect the multiple violations. For example, here the score could be a possible 15 points, up to 5 points for each violation. After each sustained violation, the points should be added together. If only one of the violations had been sustained, the original calculated score would be appropriate.

Category J: Other

This category is to be used as a catch-all. Given the rapid development of new technology and the creativity of children to abuse it, this category allows administrative flexibility for future endeavors or student conduct that does not fit into one of the previous categories.

Section 4: Offender Score

Section 4 provides a system for making numerical calculations correlating to the offender's status and personal characteristics. This section is used to evaluate the offender's status as a leader or a follower and whether the offender played a major or minor role in the conduct. This section includes information regarding whether the perpetrator engaged in obstructionist activities or exploited a position of trust. Additionally, the offender's history of disciplinary actions, school participation in **positive educational events,** and current level of supervision are all assessed. Finally, this section also measures the degree to which the offender's conduct impacted or was connected to the school's learning environment or to other students. All of these Section 4 factors are evaluated on a Likert-type scale to determine a total offender score.

Category A: Leader/Follower

Under this category, the student role in the offensive conduct is evaluated. Seriousness of offense is directly tied to the level of leadership taken by the student. Individuals that create and bring offensive cyber materials to school (in whatever fashion) should be held to a

Figure 13.5 Offender Score

Offender Score							
A	Leader Follower	0	1	2	3	4	5
B	Active/Passive Participation	0	1	2	3	4	5
C	Obstructionist's Activities	0	1	2	3	4	5
D	Exploiting Positions of Trust	0	1	2	3	4	5
E	Current Supervision	0	1	2	3	4	5
F	Prior Disciplinary Actions	0	1	2	3	4	5
G	Lack of School Participation	0	1	2	3	4	5
H	School/Student Nexus	0	1	2	3	4	5
I	School/Conduct Nexus	0	1	2	3	4	5
J	Other	0	1	2	3	4	5
		Total =					

higher level of responsibility. A leader is defined as an individual who singularly directs, guides, creates, or advances inappropriate expressions. This includes a student who

- has created materials,
- has disseminated materials, or
- has created and disseminated materials.

The point score given will depend upon the student's position of authority and participation at all levels of the expression that culminated in the disruption. For example, a student who created the materials but did not disseminate them would receive fewer points than a student who did disseminate them or directed that this be done.

An example of a leader that created, disseminated, and encouraged others to participate in the offensive conduct can be found in *Doninger.* Student Avery Doninger served as junior class secretary and student council member. She posted information on an independently publicly accessible blog and provided specific contact names and information to the community. She urged others to forward an e-mail to as many people as possible. Her blog protesting the postponement of the Jamfest caused a substantial disruption at the school. Because of her leadership role in this situation, she would be awarded a score of four or five (4 or 5).

Followers are individuals who have little role in creating or disseminating the expressions. Typically they are bystanders or supporters who follow direction or who play a minimal leadership role in the disruptive activity. An example of this is found in *Requa v. Kent School District No. 415.* Requa, along with two friends, secretly videotaped his teacher and posted the video on YouTube. Several months later, a Seattle news channel aired the video, and a substantial disruption ensued at the school. In this case, because of his joint participation in the creation of the video, Requa served in a lesser leadership role. The fact that there were three equally involved students mitigates his culpability as a singular leader. Additionally, as the news channel provided this service, Requa receives no leadership points for dissemination, but he would be awarded a score of one to two (1 to 2) for creative leadership.

Category B: Active/Passive Participation

In defining whether participation is active or passive, the degree of involvement or contribution to the disruptive activity will determine the points awarded. Students are determined to have been active participants when they directly participated in most, if not all, of the disruptive activity. For example, the two Columbine seniors, Harris and Klebold, who killed 13 people and injured 21 others, would both receive 5 points for their active participation in the massacre.

A passive participant would be a student who is not directly involved in the creation or dissemination of offensive expressions but gets involved through participation in the aftermath. These are typically students who "jump on board," spread the word, and direct class time away from instruction. These students would receive a score of 0 to 1.

Category C: Obstructionist Activities

This category includes activities where offenders attempt to hide their activity or to prevent officials from discovering their involvement. Included in this category are threatening and intimidating behaviors and anonymizing activities. For example, if an offender threatens or retaliates against those who exposed his or her inappropriate expressions, the score would be high. Attempting to silence others to avoid liability also results in a high score.

Anonymizing activities include the use of an intermediary website to hide or disguise an Internet address associated with Internet use. This would also include impersonating activities. Impersonating occurs when a student pretends to be someone else. The list of possible impersonating activities grows daily. Current methods include hacking into a victim's account, and then masquerading as the victim to send out embarrassing or hurtful messages. In *A.B. v. State of Indiana,*[39] the student impersonated the principal and posted derogatory comments. The school referred A. B.'s case to the juvenile court, as here the impersonation constituted identity deception, which is a felony offense. If a student's actions constitute a felony offense, a high score would be allocated. If the actions constitute a misdemeanor, a lower score would be assigned. If the impersonation is deemed a political speech, no sanction is permissible.

Category D: Exploiting Positions of Trust

This category involves individuals who have been entrusted with a job or responsibility using school-based technology (hardware, software, Internet access). Those individuals then utilize that higher level of access to exploit an individual or group. For example, the offender works in the school office and has access to confidential information, such as students' grades, medical history, and other personal data. The offender shares the information with others, to the detriment of the victim. This constitutes a violation of trust. Another example is when offenders play the role of a "frenemy." In this case, offenders use the victim's personal relationship to gain information to exploit, harass, or humiliate someone that trusted them.

Category E: Current Supervision

This category applies to students who are currently under supervision and working on addressing the problems that got them in trouble. It would be expected that they are on their best behavior. If they commit further violations while attending programs or receiving intervention, additional points will be added. Basically, the continued inappropriate activities express a lack of respect for the system; the greater the lack of respect, the higher the score.

Category F: Prior Disciplinary Actions

If the offender has had previous consequences for inappropriate behaviors, then this category applies. If not, the offender would be given a score of 0. It is irrelevant whether or not the prior conduct was related to cyber bullying. The importance of this category is that school officials have intervened while attempting to address negative patterns of social behavior. If by engaging in the present offense the student demonstrates a lack of amenability (has not learned from previous situations or consequences), points should be added. If the new offense shows an escalating severity of incidents, a higher score should be given. For example, the offensive behavior has escalated when the first offense involved rudeness and the later offense "creating guns and blowing heads off." Further, a graduated level of points should be given for repetition of the same offense. It is difficult to defend issuing the same consequence for repeating the same misbehavior, as doing the same ineffective thing over and over doesn't make sense. Assigning 5 points to the score makes the offender accountable for his incorrigibility.

Category G: Lack of School Participation

Offenders who willfully fail to participate in appropriate educational programs would be assigned points. Students who do not attend school and complete assignments, and who have not participated in previous administrative recommendations for remediation or interventions, would be assigned an appropriate level of points. Simply attending, with minimal evidence of "learning," would not be recognized as having completed the task and would result in a score of 1. A similar score would be assigned for passive-aggressive behavior. Students receive points for failing to do what students are supposed to do—attend classes, actively participate, be on time, and so forth.

Passive responses to participation would not be acknowledged as successfully completing the required task. For example, sitting in the required afterschool netiquette session and reading a comic book would not count for successful completion of the disciplinary action.

Category H: School/Student Nexus

School administrators may sanction only student behavior that bears a sufficient nexus to the school. Questions that should be considered include the following:

- Did the student offender bring the expression to school, causing the disruption?
- Was the expression made publicly or privately?
- Were there others who were instrumental in bringing the expression to campus?
- How and when was the expression brought to campus?
- Did the student offender **send** the bullying information to individuals directly connected to the school?
- Did the student offender specifically target school-related individuals (e.g., administrators, teachers, staff, or other students)?
- Did the student offender target them personally, professionally, or both?

If the answer to any of these questions is in the affirmative, points should be assessed. That is, if the student intentionally caused the inappropriate expression to affect the school, a high score should be assigned. For example, in *J.S. v. Blue Mountain,*[40] two eighth graders created a fictitious profile on a social networking site where they targeted the school principal. Created as a self-portrayal of the principal, the profile alluded to sexual activities, inappropriate for a professional. The girls shared the profile with 22 students. The website caused a disruption to the educational environment, because it targeted a school official and was disseminated to 22 classmates. Hence, the students would receive a high score (4 or 5) on the MATRIX. Compare this with the case of *Beidler v. North Thurston County School District,*[41] where the student created a website ridiculing a school administrator for having sex with Homer Simpson. A score of 0 would be issued for this offense, as no school disruption occurred. No one should have taken the website seriously.

Category I: School/Conduct Nexus

- What is the conduct's connection to the school?
- Is it school-sponsored speech (within the perimeter of the school, curriculum, and instruction) or is it independently created (e.g., an unofficial/unauthorized website of a school)?
- Was it the school's reaction that caused the disruption? For example, what role did the administration's reaction to the expression have in the disruption?

In *Doninger,* the student purposely designed her blog so that its effects would disrupt campus and encourage others to contact the administration. Her blatant conduct significantly disrupted the school, so she should be assigned 4 or 5 points.

In *Latour v. Riverside Beaver School District,*[42] a student posted violent lyrics on a battle rap website. Disruptive protests by other students began after the principal sanctioned the student for his rap. The student could not be sanctioned, since the battle rap was political commentary. Political commentary could only be sanctioned if the student's commentary caused a substantial disruption. Here, it was the school administrator's reactions that caused the disruptions. Hence, the student should receive a score of 0.

Category J: Other

This category is a catch-all that represents a unique situation or behavioral response not covered in the previous categories. If the administrator believes that an additional aggravating circumstance existed that was significant to the presenting conduct, use this space to award points.

Section 5: Mitigation Score

Section 5 develops numerical calculations reflecting mitigating circumstances surrounding the offender's liability for his conduct. The total from this score is subtracted from the total reached from combining the results from Section 3 (presenting offense score) and Section 4 (offender score) described above. Section 5 allows consideration for the age and cognitive and physical development level of the offender. This section also gives credit to those offenders who admit guilt, voluntarily seek treatment to address their issues, make atonement by cooperating with authorities, provide restitution, or modify their behavior in a positive manner. It also addresses the role, if any, that the victim played in the offense. Again, each of these criteria is assigned a value on a Likert-type scale, and the total is then calculated. **In this section, higher scores indicate less liability on the part of the offender.**

Figure 13.6 Mitigation Score

Mitigation Score							
A	Offender Age	0	1	2	3	4	5
B	Cognitive/Physical Development	0	1	2	3	4	5
C	Voluntarily Seeking Treatment	0	1	2	3	4	5
D	Issue Already Being Addressed	0	1	2	3	4	5
E	Admission of Guilt	0	1	2	3	4	5
F	Cooperation/Atonement	0	1	2	3	4	5
G	Restitution	0	1	2	3	4	5
H	Current Behavior	0	1	2	3	4	5
I	Victim's Role in Offense	0	1	2	3	4	5
J	Other	0	1	2	3	4	5
		Total =					

Category A: Offender Age

In the case of the age of the offender, it is assumed that the younger the offenders, the less responsible they might be for their actions. Although this line of reasoning holds merit, there are many variables related to this decision. A young, technology-savvy offender might well understand that the information posted on the Internet could potentially reach hundreds of thousands of viewers, but not understand the numeracy of hundreds of thousands. Questions to be considered might include the following:

- Did the student offenders have the moral developmental ability to predict (foresee) the outcomes of their actions?
- Did the student offenders have the cognitive developmental ability to predict the outcomes of their actions?
- Did the student offenders truly understand the seriousness and the extent of their conduct?

It is important to remember that if the student was too young to understand the meaning of the expression or was mimicking an older person's behavior, a high score would be assigned. For example a 4- or 5-year-old saying "f— you" or giving someone "the finger" might score a 5, as it could be presumed that students this young do not understand what they are doing in such instances. In contrast, in *Harper v. Poway Unified School District,*[43] the students' age is not a mitigating factor. They were old enough to be fully aware of the impact the expression "Homosexuality Is Shameful" would have on their peers. Thus they would receive a score of 0 for mitigation.

Category B: Cognitive or Physical Development

In this category, school administration is encouraged to consider cognitive and physical development as it relates to students' ability to make decisions and accept responsibility for their actions. Administrators should consider the following:

- What psychosocial issues might be contributing to the situation?
- Was the offender capable of making sufficiently sophisticated cognitive decisions as to predict the outcome?
- Was the action impulsive and spontaneous, or was it a planned premeditated action?

A score of 0 would be assigned to situations similar to that in the *J.S. v. Bethlehem* case. In this situation, a student depicted the teacher's face dripping in blood and morphing into Hitler. An example of a higher score, a 4 or 5, would be found in the situation where a student instantly forwarded a nude picture (sexting) of a classmate to others. In essence, the greater the level of planning or lack of impulse control, the fewer the number of points awarded.

Category C: Voluntarily Seeking Treatment

Did the offender or the offender's parents or legal guardian(s) suggest a course of treatment that would reduce or eliminate the possibility of future misconduct? To what degree were specific plans made regarding the treatment? In other words, have treatment facilities or services been identified, appointments been made or held? This category recognizes steps made by or on behalf of the students to self-correct their attitudes, beliefs, or behavior. If after being caught the student volunteers to make amends or attend an intervention program, 5 points should be awarded. The intensity of the intervention should be considered when allocating points. For example, a one-time appointment would receive fewer points than placement in a residential program.

Category D: Issue Already Being Addressed

If the underlying reason the student committed the offense was tied to something the student was working on at the time of the offense, such as drug treatment, gang involvement, or counseling, this should be considered a mitigating factor. It is possible for regression to occur. Some realization of this should be reflected in the scoring. Behavioral changes take time, and thus expectations of perfection should be recognized as unrealistic—setbacks might occur.

The essence of the educational environment is one that supports student learning—even in areas involving changing behaviors. Multiple opportunities to change behavior should be weighed against a student's steady consistent progress. Minor fallbacks are to be expected. Up to 5 points might be given when steady improvements or progress have been made by the offending student.

Consideration might also be given to punishment or consequences originating outside the school. For example, if the student is receiving parental or court-ordered discipline, points should be allocated.

Category E: Admission of Guilt

One of the basic tenets of creating behavioral change is that before change will occur, offenders must admit their guilt in an offense and acknowledge that they have a problem that requires intervention. The belief is that if student offenders genuinely take ownership or responsibility for their behavior and its underlining causes(s), they are less likely to reoffend. Students who admit their involvement early in the investigation would receive more points than those who admit later or not at all. Total failure to take responsibility for the offense would garner 0 points. Be aware that there is a difference between admitting guilt or responsibility and acquiescing to an inevitable finding of guilt.

Category F: Cooperation or Atonement

A student offender who works with administration in resolving situations or correcting the damage done should be recognized. This category gives cooperative students points for their assistance. When students truly apologize, make amends, or atone, they should receive points reflective of their actions. For example, a student who takes down an offending website, makes genuine face-to-face apologies to all victims, makes public corrections, or apologizes should receive atonement points. An additional consideration is the degree to which the student self-identified an acceptable solution. Be aware that **actions speak louder than words.** Thus, a verbal apology with a change in behavior (e.g., turning a shirt inside out to hide offensive words or graphics, deleting offensive photos or comments from a website) would support allocations of 3 to 5 points.

Category G: Restitution

Another indicator of lessons learned involves making restitution. Restitution can be made through financial payments or through services offered. Student offenders who volunteer their time or other resources to make victims whole should be rewarded. Be aware that student offenders cannot "buy off" their responsibilities. The student **must** be seen as being actively engaged in the restitution process. A student offender who devotes time to lead or participate in restorative justice programs would receive points depending upon the level of commitment and involvement. This category also includes community service, nonrequired service-learning time, and volunteer activities.

Category H: Current Behavior

The current behavior category recognizes that a student may make a mistake and instantly recognize the error. If the student offender's behavior changes such that the current behavior is acceptable, credit should be given. For example, a student who violates the school's AUP by creating a derogatory web-based commentary on a social networking site while at school, and who then becomes a spokesperson and model student for following AUP, would receive mitigation points. **The key to the number of assigned points will vary depending upon how long the current behavior has lasted.** For example, one week of good behavior might not get any points, while one month would merit some points.

Category I: Victim's Role in Offense

School administrators are aware that students are social beings. Human interactions do not occur within a vacuum. There are times when the victim plays a role in the offense. Although the student offender's response is always wrong, the victim may bear some responsibility. When this happens, this category allows the student offender some relief. The amount of points awarded in this category should be both proportional and reasonable in light of the victim's contribution to the offense. Caution should be noted that the victim remains the victim and should not be further victimized in order to downsize the student offender's responsibility. For example, when two students who have been a couple break up, they might send hurtful or hateful e-mails to each other. A student offender would take it the next level by placing sexting photos on the former partner's page on a social networking site. Things escalate on campus, and the pair's break-up disrupts several classes. Even though both were guilty initially, one student took the offense to a more negative level. The student offender might receive a point recognizing the victim's role.

Category J: Other

This category is a catch-all that allows for a unique situation or behavioral response not covered in the previous categories. An administrator who believes that an additional mitigating circumstance existed that was significant to the presenting situations can use this space to award points.

Section 6: Evaluation Score

Section 6, the final MATRIX section, combines the scores from Sections 3, 4, and 5. This combined score reflects the level of severity of the presenting conduct, the culpability and characteristics of the offender, and the effect of the electronic aggression on the victims and the institutions. The final score gives educators a numerical basis for leveling the appropriate sanctions.

The score in Section 3 includes the impact of the **presenting conduct** on individual victims and the school environment. A total score is created by adding the points awarded in categories A-J of this section.

The **offender's score** is calculated in Section 4. The offender's score includes a total point assessment for the list of objective factors characterizing the offender from an aggravating perspective.

In Section 5, a **mitigation score** is totaled, giving credit for the objective factors that mitigate against the offender's culpability or militate against harsh sanctioning for the cyber bullying incident.

The presenting offense score plus the offender's score minus the mitigation score results in a total sanctioning score (see Figure 13.7). **The higher the sanctioning score, the harsher the consequences.** Furthermore, high scores for any individual item will influence whether a school system should engage in education, rehabilitation, or redress of the problematic circumstance.

Figure 13.7 Evaluation Score

Presenting Offense Score								Offender Score								Mitigation Score							
A	Seriousness Category	0	1	2	3	4	5	A	Leader Follower	0	1	2	3	4	5	A	Offender Age	0	1	2	3	4	5
B	Vicious/ Heinous Conduct	0	1	2	3	4	5	B	Active/Passive Participation	0	1	2	3	4	5	B	Cognitive/ Physical Development	0	1	2	3	4	5
C	Duration	0	1	2	3	4	5	C	Obstructionist's Activities	0	1	2	3	4	5	C	Voluntarily Seeking Treatment	0	1	2	3	4	5
D	Number of Victims	0	1	2	3	4	5	D	Exploiting Positions of Trust	0	1	2	3	4	5	D	Issue Already Being Addressed	0	1	2	3	4	5
E	Victim Injury Level	0	1	2	3	4	5	E	Current Supervision	0	1	2	3	4	5	E	Admission of Guilt	0	1	2	3	4	5
F	Victim Vulnerability	0	1	2	3	4	5	F	Prior Disciplinary Actions	0	1	2	3	4	5	F	Cooperation/ Atonement	0	1	2	3	4	5
G	Gang Involvement	0	1	2	3	4	5	G	Lack of School Participation	0	1	2	3	4	5	G	Restitution	0	1	2	3	4	5
H	Under the Influence	0	1	2	3	4	5	H	School/Student Nexus	0	1	2	3	4	5	H	Current Behavior	0	1	2	3	4	5
I	Multiple Violations	0	1–5	1–5	1–5	1–5	1–5	I	School/Conduct Nexus	0	1	2	3	4	5	I	Victim's Role in Offense	0	1	2	3	4	5
J	Other	0	1	2	3	4	5	J	Other	0	1	2	3	4	5	J	Other	0	1	2	3	4	5
		Total =								Total =								Total =					

Presenting Offense Score	+	Offender Score	–	Mitigation Score	= ________ Total
Date and Description of Actual Disposition Imposed:				Worksheet Prepared By:	

General Guidelines for the School Sanctioning Worksheet

The School Sanctioning Worksheet is meant to function as a guideline for school administrators. **Each of the sections need NOT be scored.** Scoring will depend upon the information available at the time the administrator is investigating or deciding sanctions. Some of the information will not be available or may not be appropriate for inclusion on the worksheet. For example, the student's level of cooperation, current supervision, or gang involvement, or the role of the victim, might not be known at the time that the MATRIX is being completed. Expediency may require that administration disregard those sections. **The MATRIX is a GUIDELINE for decision making, not a mandatory obligation.**

The worksheet should be completed for each reported incident of cyber bullying. A reported incident of cyber bullying is defined as one or more presenting offenses committed in the course of a single event. Accurate completion of the worksheet enables uniform guidance for sanctions and documents the objective decision-making process.

No Double Counting

It can be very tempting to score or count the same variable under more than one criterion. Doing so skews the MATRIX and moves the results toward capriciousness. For example, if the age of the offender is an issue and points are awarded in one category, using age again in another category would be wrong. **A single variable should NOT dominate the MATRIX.**

Team Decision-Making Process

Many cyber bullying incidents involve multiple school personnel; this can include teachers, counselors, technicians, staff, principals, administrators, and legal counsel. Typically each views the situation from a different yet important perspective that may be overlooked or not adequately considered by others. Thus, in cyber bullying situations, it is quite useful to use a team approach while completing the MATRIX Sanctioning Worksheet. When school personnel reach a group consensus, the points assigned will reflect a more complete picture and will be less arbitrary and more consistent within a school or district. The richness of their discussions would also create homogeneous understandings of the MATRIX factors that would support their defense if any litigation were to arise from the case.

Recommendations

The MATRIX is a comprehensive assessment tool that encourages administrators to evaluate and document instances of cyber bullying. It provides a visible format for identifying factors, issues, trends, and concerns that influence appropriate decision making. The MATRIX contains objective, not subjective, factors from which neutral, unbiased, and nonemotional decisions can be reached. Its strength lies in the thoroughness, practicality, and complexity with which problems are evaluated. The MATRIX is intended to complement school districts' preexisting policies, not to replace them. As a result of following the MATRIX guidelines, administrators will have documentation as well as a rationale for their outcomes. The information documented on the MATRIX will prove helpful when defending or explaining the administration's decision to student offenders, parents/family, school lawyers, and/or the courts. The MATRIX should be considered a continuous work in progress. As student offenders create new challenges to administrators, the worksheet should be reevaluated and/or updated.

Notes

1. LaVine v. Blaine School District, 257 F.3d 981, 992 (9th Cir. 2001); *cert. denied*, 536 U.S. 959, 992 (2002).
2. Yap v. Oceanside Union Free School District, 303 F. Supp. 2d 284 (E.D. N.Y. 2004).
3. *Id.* at 295.
4. Lovell by and through Lovell v. Poway Unified School District, 90 F.3d 367, 372 (9th Cir. 1996).
5. NAACP Legal Defense and Education Fund. (n.d.). *Dismantling the school-to-prison pipeline.* New York: Author. Retrieved from http://www.naacpldf.org/content/pdf/pipeline/Dismantling_the_School_to_Prison_Pipeline.pdf.
6. Advancement Project and The Civil Rights Project at Harvard University. (2000). *Opportunities suspended: The devastating consequences of zero tolerance and school discipline policies.* As cited in NAACP, *supra* note 5 at 13.
7. Ward et al. v. Rock Against Racism, 491 U.S. 781, 791 (1989).
8. Nuxoll v. Indian Prairie School District #204, 523 F.3d 668, 672 (7th Cir. 2008).
9. Saxe v. State College Area School District, 240 F.3d 200, 210 (3d Cir. 2001).
10. Sypniewski v. Warren Hills Regional Board of Education, 307 F.3d 243 (3d Cir. 2002).
11. Chalifoux v. New Caney Independent School District, 976 F. Supp. 659 (S.D. Tex, 1997).
12. Morse v. Frederick, 551 U.S. 393, 425 (2007) (Alito, J. concurring).

13. Hazelwood School District v. Kuhlmeier, 484 U.S. 260, 271 (1988).
14. Bethel School District No. 403 v. Fraser, 478 U.S. 675, 681 (1986).
15. Hazelwood, 484 U.S. at 266.
16. Fraser, 478 U.S. at 681.
17. *Id.* at 681.
18. *Id.* at 683.
19. Hazelwood, 484 U.S. at 284.
20. Killion v. Franklin Regional School Board, 136 F. Supp. 2d 446, 453 (W.D. Pa. 2001).
21. Hazelwood, 484 U.S. at 270–271.
22. Saxe v. State College Area School District, 240 F.3d 200, 214 (3d Cir. 2001).
23. Morse v. Frederick, 551 U.S. 393, 425 (2007) (Alito, J., concurring).
24. Ponce v. Socorro Independent School District, 508 F.3d 765, 771 (5th Cir. 2007)
25. Davis v. Monroe County Board of Education, 526 U.S. 629, 652 (1999).
26. 42 U.S.C. 2000e-2(a)(1). Oncale v. Sundowner Offshore Services, Inc., 523 U.S. 75, 80 (1998).
27. Requa v. Kent School District No. 415, 492 F. Supp. 2d 1272, 73–74 (W.D. Wa. 2007).
28. O.Z. v. Board of Trustees of Long Beach Unified School District, 2008 LEXIS 110409 (C.D. Cal., 2008).
29. J.C. v. Beverly Hills Unified School District, 2010 LEXIS 54481 (C.D. Cal. 2010).
30. Doninger v. Niehoff, 514 F. Supp. 2d 199 (2007), *affirmed* 527 F.3d 41, 52 (2d Cir. 2008).
31. L.W. v. Toms River Regional Schools, 2005 WL 3299837 (N.J. sup. A.D., Dec. 7, 2005).
32. Lowery v. Euverard, 497 F.3d 584 (6th Cir. 2007), *cert. denied* 2008 U.S. LEXIS 6449 (2008).
33. J.S. ex rel. H.S. v. Bethlehem Area School District, 569 Pa. 638, 646, 807 A. 2d 847, 852 (Pa. 2002).
34. Klein v. Smith, 635 F. Supp. 1440, 1442 (D. Me. 1986).
35. Chalifoux v. New Caney Independent School District, 976 F. Supp. 659 (S.D. Tex. 1997).
36. Sypniewski v. Warren Hills Regional Board of Education, 307 F.3d 243 (3d Cir. 2002), *cert. denied* 38 U.S. 1033 (2003).
37. *Id.* at 247.
38. *Id.* at 247.
39. A.B. v. State of Indiana, 863 N.E. 2d 1212 (Ind. Ct. App. 2007).
40. J.S. et al. v. Blue Mountain School District, 593 F.3d 286 (3d Cir. 2010), *vacated, rehearing en banc* (pending 6/3/2010), 2010 LEXIS 7342 (3d Cir. Apr. 9, 2010).
41. Beidler v. North Thurston County School District, No. 99-2-00236-6 (Thurston Cty. Super. Ct. July 18, 2000).
42. Latour v. Riverside Beaver School District, 2005 LEXIS 35919 (W.D. Pa. 2005).
43. Harper v. Poway Unified School District, 445 F.3d 1166 (9th Cir. 2006), *vacated* 549 U.S. 1262 (2007).

Glossary

Acceptable use policies (AUPs). Contractual agreements among school districts, students, and parents setting forth acceptable practices for decorum and equipment usage.

Aggravating circumstances. Factors that compound or worsen the extent or effect of cyber aggressive conduct. Such factors include the duration, intensity, and viciousness of the cyber bullying activity as well as the motivation and impact on victims.

Anonymizing. Hiding behind an intermediary website or anonymizer to prevent identification of the source.

Bash boards. Internet discussion forums where people post highly critical statements, racial comments, condemning remarks, or gossip about others. Remarks typically focus on core characteristics or personality traits.

Battle rap. A genre of music whereby artists try to outdo one another by depicting violent imagery and coarse vulgar language with no intent to harm.

Bystanders. Onlookers present at an event or who receive online messages but do not actually contribute to the discussion or website materials. Bystanders include those who merely forward information to other nonparticipants. Although bystanders remain on the sidelines of cyber bullying, they contribute to the effects by witnessing the events and experiencing the emotional fallout created by the aggressive expressions. Bystanders often require psychosocial intervention due to the trauma caused from experiencing cyber bullying behavior.

Columbine. The site of the April 20, 1999, school massacre in Columbine, Colorado, where 12 students and one teacher were killed and 24 other students were wounded. The phrase "going Columbine" commonly connotes death as a result of one or more students shooting other students and school personnel. The phrase is an off-handed expression depicting a desire to cause school violence similar to the phrase "going postal" intimating killing individuals in the workplace.

Common law. A basis of law premised on the belief that similar situations should be treated the same. Common law is a legal system without a statutory basis or an executive mandate that gives precedential weight to previous judicial written opinions. Past opinions bind or dictate (establish precedent for) future opinions. Judges develop the common law as situations arise. Therefore, the common law changes or advances over time based on traditional jusrisdictional customs and mores.

Communications Decency Act (CDA). An act designed by Congress in 1996 to regulate pornography (indecency and obscenity) over the Internet (Title V of the Telecommunications Act of 1996, Pub. L. No. 104–104, 110 Stat. 133 (1996), amended and codified at scattered sections of 47 U.S.C.). Specifically, the act criminalized the intentional transmission of "obscene or indecent" materials to persons under 18. In 1997, in *ACLU v. Reno* (929 F. Supp. 824 (E.D. Pa. 1996), *affirmed* 521 U.S. 844 (1997)), the Supreme Court held that the indecency portion of the act violated the First Amendment. Parents should decide what materials are appropriate or indecent for their children. In 2003, Congress amended the CDA by removing the indecency provisions. The Supreme Court indirectly upheld the constitutionality of the new statute in 2006 in the case of *Nitke v. Gonzalez* (413 F. Supp. 2d 262 (S.D. N.Y. 2005), *affirmed* 547 U.S. 1015 (2006)).

Cyber bullying. The use of technology to harass, humiliate, hurt, or embarrass another. Not all forms of cyber bullying are illegal or sanctionable by school districts.

Cyber bullying by proxy. Convincing others to send hate or flame mail to the victim and then, when the victim responds in an inappropriate way, forwarding the response to an authority figure who punishes the victim.

Cyber stalking. Sending threatening messages of harm that are highly intimidating, causing victims to fear for their safety.

Deliberate indifference. Acting with total disregard for the consequences of one's actions. The term requires that an individual has made a conscious choice among options available and has chosen to consciously or recklessly act regardless of the outcome. Deliberate indifference requires more than mere negligence.

De minimis. Minimal or with very little significance or importance.

Denigrating. Dissing (disrespecting) someone online by posting cruel statements, gossip, or rumors to destroy or damage his or her reputation.

Due Process Clause. A provision within the Fourteenth Amendment that protects rights of individuals and corporations. Due process includes both procedural and substantive protections before deprivations of life, liberty, or property may be imposed.

Duty to protect. The legal responsibility of a school district to intervene and afford protection for students under its care. Typically, schools have no legal obligation to protect students from peer-to-peer harm. However, if there is a systemic violence, then schools may be required to intervene and not act with deliberate indifference to the peer-to-peer harm in certain situations.

Eleventh Amendment. The constitutional provision that provides that "The Judicial power of the United States shall not be construed to extend to any suit in law or equity, commenced or prosecuted against one of the United States by Citizens of another State, or by Citizens or Subjects of any Foreign State." This amendment is interpreted as granting immunity in the federal courts to each state from lawsuits by citizens of its own state, other states, foreign countries, or citizens of foreign countries.

Elementary and Secondary Education Act (ESEA). An act that established equality in educational access and standards for accountability. In 2002, this act was amended and became the No Child Left Behind (NCLB) legislation.

Exclusion or Boycott. Intentionally excluding a person from an online group, chat room, game, or IM buddies list.

Fighting words. Words that intentionally provoke a specific group to immediately react in a hostile manner.

First Amendment. The constitutional provision that prohibits legislation abridging freedom of speech. Although no right is absolute, the limitations to free expression are strictly and narrowly defined and enforced.

Flaming. Posting or sending extremely nasty electronic messages in a public forum to inflame or enrage the recipient. Flaming typically results in retaliatory online fighting.

Foreseeability. The predictability or natural and probable consequences of one's actions. Harm is foreseeable when a reasonable person would anticipate or expect such a result from certain behavior.

Frenemy. An offender who uses a personal relationship with a victim to gain or gather information to exploit, harass, or humiliate someone who has trusted him or her.

Happy slapping. A physical attack or provocation of an unsuspecting target. An accomplice records the incident and posts it online, distributes it electronically, or shares with friends. The intention of happy slapping is to record a real-life drama.

Harassment. Repeatedly sending offensive, rude, and insulting messages.

Hate mail. Messages exposing prejudices, including those involving race and sex.

Impersonation. Masquerading as the victim, the perpetrator posts messages containing embarrassing or insulting information with the intent to damage a friendship or reputation. Readers believe that the victim wrote the posts.

Impinge-on-the-right-of-others test. The test created by the Supreme Court in *Tinker v. Des Moines Independent Community School District* that allows censorship of student expression under the First Amendment. The test allows censorship when the expression actually interferes with a student's right to educational benefits or substantially detracts from the learning environment. Typically this test is limited to those expressions that attack core characteristics of race, ethnicity, religion, gender, sexual orientation, or disability.

Imprimatur. The official authorization or sanctioning approval by a school.

Immunity. A legal status that immunizes individuals or entities from lawsuits. The concept removes them from the potential of liability and, in essence, places them above or free from legal obligations, including liability for damages or harm.

In loco parentis. English translation of this Latin term means "in place of the parent." In school settings, the doctrine has come to mean that schools stand in place of the parents with regard to children under their charge. Under the common law of England, schools were responsible for both the educational and moral development of school children. Hence the school's authority over school children at school was as extensive as the parents' authority. However, since the children's rights movement of the 1960s and recent Supreme Court cases, public schools no longer stand as parents over school children. School children retain their own constitutional rights (within limits), and parents maintain authority over their children's moral education.

Internet polling. Participating in online polls that critically rate a victim's physical appearance or other characteristics.

Mitigating circumstances. Events or factors that lesson or reduce liability for one's actions. In terms of cyber bullying, such factors include cognitive development, age, atonement, and current behavioral status.

Netiquette. A term that evolved from "network etiquette"; it refers to a set of social guidelines that encourage civil interaction over electronic technology. The term implies proper manners to be used when communicating online.

Nexus. A legal term meaning causal connection or linkage between two events. In terms of cyber bullying sanctioning, a sufficient association or relationship must be demonstrated between the student's expression and the harm caused to another student or the disruption to the institution before punishment may inure.

Outing and phishing. Engaging or encouraging victims into online conversations so that the victim is tricked into revealing sensitive or confidential information. The perpetrator then viciously forwards the embarrassing information to others, allegedly as a "joke."

Overbreadth. A legal doctrine that applies to regulation of free speech. Regulation that is overbroad prohibits both restrainable and nonrestrainable speech. Policies or regulations that attempt to broadly or extensively censor content of expressions are often found to violate this doctrine. School policies that attempt to regulate expressions invoking "ill will" are generally illustrative of an overly broad policy, because the term "ill will" includes both sanctionable and nonsanctionable behaviors.

Poking. To reach out and virtually touch someone online. For example, poking a friend on a social networking site (such as Facebook, MySpace, or Bebo) causes the friend to receive a message that he or she has been poked. Not all pokes are harmless.

Polling. Creating polls on websites at which site visitors vote on undesirable characteristics, such as who is the fattest, ugliest, sluttiest, geekiest, and so forth.

Precedent. A legal doctrine that requires courts to follow the previous practices or rulings of superior courts.

Presenting conduct. Refers to the categories of cyber bullying conduct corresponding to criminal offenses or legal precedent.

Procedural due process. A provision within the Fourteenth Amendment that requires a process or series of steps to be undertaken before the government may deprive individuals or corporations of life, liberty, or property. Typically, procedural due process includes such measures as notice of impending deprivation and the right to respond, have counsel, or appeal. All of these measures must be taken in a meaningful and timely manner.

Proximate cause. The legal cause of harm. Harm or injury that results as a natural consequence of conduct is found to support legal causation. Proximate cause of an injury includes conduct that *but for* its occurrence, no injury would have resulted. To determine proximate cause, many courts consider whether the conduct played a substantial role (though not necessarily the only role) in producing the negative consequence.

Public forums. Spaces where persons may openly express their opinions. Typically public forums include public streets, parks, and other traditional open forums. Since schools are not deemed public forums, school officials may regulate the content of students' expressions.

Rational basis analysis. A judicial standard of review that determines whether censorship of an expression is based upon a reasonable and legitimate government interest or is an arbitrary and capricious decision.

School-to-prison pipeline. A belief that students who are prosecuted are funneled on a path to prison.

Sexting. Posting an embarrassing, sexually explicit photo on the Internet or sending sexually explicit text messages or photos on a cell phone.

Sovereign immunity. The Eleventh Amendment's legal protection that prevents state or federal governmental entities from being sued without their consent. The doctrine developed from the belief that the king could do no wrong; therefore, he could not be challenged.

Spam. Flooding the Internet with multiple copies of the same message to voluntary and involuntary recipients.

Substantial and material disruption test. A test created by the Supreme Court in *Tinker v. Des Moines Independent Community School District* that allows censorship of student expression under the First Amendment. The test requires more than ordinary disruption but less than complete chaos.

Substantive due process. A part of the Fourteenth Amendment's Due Process Clause. Substantive due process affords protection from deprivations of unenumerated rights, including parental, privacy, and marriage rights. For example, the right to bodily integrity, the right to life, and the right to raise one's children as one chooses fall within this protection.

Territoriality. A term that defines a border or a limitation of jurisdiction. With regard to cyber expressions, territoriality refers to the geographic area wherein an expression originated or was received. School districts have jurisdiction over expressions that are made within their schoolyard gates or that detract substantially and materially from the educational process.

Threat. A deliberately posted statement that indicates intent to harm another person. Only threats of serious, imminent harm may be sanctioned.

Title IX. A title of the Education Amendments of 1972 that states, "No person in the United States shall, on the basis of sex, be excluded from participation in, be denied the benefits of, or be subjected to discrimination under any education program or activity receiving Federal financial assistance." Most commonly, Title IX is discussed in terms of its impact on athletics, but it covers all educational activities (band, science clubs, cheerleading, etc.) and access to their benefits.

Trolling. Intentionally posting messages that provoke or bait victims into "flaming" or fighting. Typically the messages relate to material that is sensitive to the victims.

True threats. Expressions communicated directly to another person that are interpreted as serious expressions of an intention to inflict bodily harm upon or to take the life of the target.

Index

The Corwin logo—a raven striding across an open book—represents the union of courage and learning. Corwin is committed to improving education for all learners by publishing books and other professional development resources for those serving the field of PreK–12 education. By providing practical, hands-on materials, Corwin continues to carry out the promise of its motto: **"Helping Educators Do Their Work Better."**

The MATRIX: School Sanctioning Worksheet

Cyber Bullying MATRIX: School Sanctioning Worksheet©	**Student Name** Last: First: Middle:	Date of Birth (DOB): Phone Number:	Sex:
	Parent/Guardian:	Phone Number:	Grade Level:
	Parent/Guardian:	Phone Number:	School District Number:
	Legal Representative:	Phone Number:	
Offender—Date(s) Contacted/Summary:			
Parent(s)—Date(s) Contacted/Summary:			
Legal Rep(s)—Date(s) Contacted/Summary:			
Victim 1—Date(s) Contacted/Summary:		DOB: Sex:	Grade Level:

Presenting Conduct	Date and Explanation
A. Criminal Civil Conduct Outside First Amendment Protection	
B. Acceptable Use Policy (AUP) Violation(s)	
C. Substantial Material Disruptions	
D. Interference With Rights of Others (including Title IX, ADA)	
E. Lewd/Vulgar/Indecent/Plainly Offensive Speech	
F. Anti–Legitimate Pedagogical Concerns (school's imprimatur)	
G. Anti–Social Civic Values	
H. Netiquette Violations (protected by First Amendment)	

Presenting Offense Score								Offender Score								Mitigation Score							
A	Seriousness Category	0	1	2	3	4	5	A	Leader Follower	0	1	2	3	4	5	A	Offender Age	0	1	2	3	4	5
B	Vicious/Heinous Conduct	0	1	2	3	4	5	B	Active/Passive Participation	0	1	2	3	4	5	B	Cognitive/Physical Development	0	1	2	3	4	5
C	Duration	0	1	2	3	4	5	C	Obstructionist's Activities	0	1	2	3	4	5	C	Voluntarily Seeking Treatment	0	1	2	3	4	5
D	Number of Victims	0	1	2	3	4	5	D	Exploiting Positions of Trust	0	1	2	3	4	5	D	Issue Already Being Addressed	0	1	2	3	4	5
E	Victim Injury Level	0	1	2	3	4	5	E	Current Supervision	0	1	2	3	4	5	E	Admission of Guilt	0	1	2	3	4	5
F	Victim Vulnerability	0	1	2	3	4	5	F	Prior Disciplinary Actions	0	1	2	3	4	5	F	Cooperation/Atonement	0	1	2	3	4	5
G	Gang Involvement	0	1	2	3	4	5	G	Lack of School Participation	0	1	2	3	4	5	G	Restitution	0	1	2	3	4	5
H	Under the Influence	0	1	2	3	4	5	H	School/Student Nexus	0	1	2	3	4	5	H	Current Behavior	0	1	2	3	4	5
I	Multiple Violations	0	1–5	1–5	1–5	1–5	1–5	I	School/Conduct Nexus	0	1	2	3	4	5	I	Victim's Role in Offense	0	1	2	3	4	5
J	Other	0	1	2	3	4	5	J	Other	0	1	2	3	4	5	J	Other	0	1	2	3	4	5
		Total =								Total =								Total =					

Presenting Offense Score +	Offender Score –	Mitigation Score = ____________ Total
Date and Description of Actual Disposition Imposed:		Worksheet Prepared By:

Caveat

The MATRIX provides an objective framework within which to structure a sanctioning decision. It does not dictate specific sanctions and should be used as a guide only. **The MATRIX is advisory, and its use is voluntary.** School administrators must consider what is an appropriate sanction based on community standards, the policies of regional offices of education, and specific state legislative directives. If any discrepancies arise between school or state policies and the manual's recommendations, always defer to independent legal counsel. Decisions to act or refrain from acting should not be determined on the basis of this information without seeking legal advice. **The MATRIX is intended to complement a school district's preexisting decision-making practices, not to replace them.**

The MATRIX: School Sanctioning Worksheet